Teacher Candidate Problem-Solving Engagement Styles: LIBRE Model Self-Management Analysis

Teacher Candidate Problem-Solving Engagement Styles: LIBRE Model Self-Management Analysis

Norma S. Guerra

INFORMATION AGE PUBLISHING, INC.
Charlotte, NC • www.infoagepub.com

Library of Congress Cataloging-In-Publication Data

The CIP data for this book can be found on the Library of Congress website (loc.gov).

Paperback: 978-1-64802-736-9
Hardcover: 978-1-64802-737-6
E-Book: 978-1-64802-738-3

Copyright © 2022 Information Age Publishing Inc.

All rights reserved. No part of this publication may be reproduced, stored in a retrieval system, or transmitted, in any form or by any means, electronic, mechanical, photocopying, microfilming, recording or otherwise, without written permission from the publisher.

Printed in the United States of America

CONTENTS

Preface vii

Introduction: Creating a New Space xiii

SECTION 1
IDENTITY FACETS WITHIN
PROBLEM-SOLVING ENGAGEMENT STYLES

1. Attention: When, Where, and Why: The Construct of Attention 3

2. The LIBRE Problem-Solving Model Conceptualized 11

3. Engagement Style is the Combination of Initial and Sustained
   Attention 21

4. An Ecological Look at Identity and Resilience
   Intersectionality: APA Multicultural Model 31

SECTION 2
ILLUSTRATIONS OF ENGAGEMENT STYLES

5. Participants and Research Plan 41

6. Case Study: First Generation Latina Female 51

7. Case Study of a Male: Multicultural 73

vi • CONTENTS

SECTION 3
ENGAGEMENT STYLE IMPLICATIONS
ON SELF-MANAGEMENT AND DEVELOPMENT

8. Ecological Multicultural Model 91

9. Community-of-Self from an Action Research Lens 99

10. Initial and Sustained Attention 107

Glossary 113

PREFACE

Welcome educators. Preparing teachers is a thought-provoking enterprise. Today's aspiring teachers often face unstated challenges embedded within the profession. Changes occur at all levels. Social justice is a major consideration in a world of diversity; increasing numbers of Black, Latinx, Asian, and other ethnic groups are the majority community make-up in today's public-schools. Demographic classroom shifts offer opportunity and challenge. Pupils, like curriculum, are often presented as one dimensional. This is not a working model. For example, the mismatch between the novice teacher, who is not yet secure in professional self-identity roles, and the responsibilities placed on that teacher to manage all classroom pupils' social emotional development, behavior, and content learning. The teacher's primary goal is survival for the day while the pupils' goal is just wanting to fit in. These goal mismatches will lead toward distinct outcomes. Pupils do not learn from teachers who are not invested; similarly, the multiple educational changes contributing to teachers' insecurities, often leave the teacher feeling alone and not supported. This combination of demand and change introduce the need for new teacher skills. This book is about self-engaged problem-solving as a learned personal investment toward regulated adaptability; a skill that assists with negotiated movement from one social setting to the next. So, what would that look like? To illustrate, let us take a trained science teacher with strong social and emotional skills, and the security to adapt to specific pupils' needs; the

---

Teacher Candidate Problem-Solving Engagement Styles:
LIBRE Model Self-Management Analysis, pages vii–xii.
Copyright © 2022 by Information Age Publishing
www.infoagepub.com
All rights of reproduction in any form reserved.

teacher assumes a self-managed responsibility for the pupils. The teacher adjusts the instructional pace and content with examples to offer more than the scripted science curriculum, this teaching approach offers a whole person learning experience. This teacher adapts the curriculum to meet pupil, behavior, cognitive understanding, and social emotional need. The teachers intentionally self-monitor "self in the classroom" as a self-awareness checkpoint to their pupils' engagement, and classroom attendance and expectations. Together the teacher with the pupils defines curricular learning. The teacher focuses on the learning, understanding of the pupils, and their experiences. This orientation shifts instruction to an informal assessment, and agile adjustment so that the pupils, their personal and class community needs, and their learning experiences have shared developmental goals. With this approach, teachers attend the classroom to teach-in-community with demonstrable skills toward outcome success.

Professional agility makes identifying environmental cues critical. Teacher candidates need an understanding of contextual signals (understanding of the environment) to be able to adjust their pupils' learning experience. There are skills involved in analyzing teaching settings, student needs, and self-awareness. Similarly, self-managed adaptive teaching approaches require teachers to embrace *self and the management of change*; these are skills that are not often found within teacher preparation curriculum. The purpose of this text is to explore teacher candidate identity development as self-managed investment.

I begin with *self-awareness*, defining it as the initial role of identity from which the management of social exchanges emerge. To illustrate, consider the teacher candidate's skill in attending to *self* and how it will extend as he interacts with school systems and/or students from different cultures. If he is insecure of his identity, he is likely to be reserved in extending himself to interact with persons who could be perceived as a risk to his success and/or safety. Thus, there are two sides to this self-awareness skill; (1) identity investment to understand who you are and how you think and feel as you move from one moment to another, and (2) contextual investment, awareness of how to interact within distinct environments. To begin this discussion, I offer two questions: How do environmental/contextual cues work to protect and facilitate resiliency? How does one develop self-awareness and attentiveness needed to assist teachers in their successful development?

Let's begin with a story. Identifying contextual cues is similar to reading a map or receiving direction. For instance, you decide to go to a restaurant that you have never been to before. Your friend tells you that the food is great, yet you have no idea how to find the restaurant or how similar your taste preference is to your friend's. You decide to take the recommendation and ask for directions, landmarks, and other cues that will assist you in locating the restaurant. Once you have the directions, more questions arise. What is the restaurant's environment? Do you need to dress-up or is it a casual eatery? Your next series of questions include whether the restaurant accepts cash and/or credit cards, and if you need to make a reservation. This information is foundational for you to have a positive dining experience. The same detail must be considered when assuming a student role. Learning how to attend to the classroom environment has impacts just like taking the wrong street to the restaurant. Neither the learning environment nor the student role are one dimensional. If one has an understanding of self and expectations that may be associated with the learning environment, this will allow for self-adjustment to be able to navigate the unknown. All persons have environmental foundations (a home or landing space where they feel comfortable to be genuine) that contribute to how they interact with their respective environments. *Identity* develops from contextual interactions which offer cues or indicators to who one is, where one originated from, and the environmental influences that are found in self-defined respected values.

Higher educational institutions have a core value to teach students to be higher order thinkers, problem-solvers, advocates, the leaders of tomorrow. Degree programs are designed to teach the skills warranted for professional success; to become workforce trailblazers. Disconnects occur as university goals collide with students' goals that may not align or vary with that of the institution. Understanding contextual cues assists the student with self-adjustments that will be required to learn, problem-solve, and develop critical thinking. There is complexity in the learning experience.

Similarly, students aspiring to teach have environmental opportunities and/or obstacles that vary and contribute to or compromise their learning and teaching. Self-awareness is an asset that can be refined to assist how they view self in interaction with their learning environments. The point at hand is that teacher candidates have within themselves the opportunity to become skilled in self-awareness and self-management to increase their resilience in moving across different environments. Their social awareness skill can be developed along with their self-awareness and management. Relational skills are an accompanying critical asset for teachers to have as they work in social settings. These are all social emotional learning (SEL) skills that teachers are now required to monitor with their pupils. Proposed here is a teacher candidate requisite of *self-investment* to efficiently manage personal and professional school, career, and life decisions. This involves problem-solving skill development. The Collaboration for Academic, Social, and Emotional Learning (CASEL) years of research has resulted in the compilation of five specific social emotional learning (SEL) domains to address competencies that contribute to social community-building. They include *self-awareness, self-management, social awareness, relational skills,* and *responsible decision-making* (CASEL, 1994). Problem-solving is the conduit that facilitates responsible decision-making.

The LIBRE problem-solving model is the instrument used to illustrate how the teacher candidate's words and attention can be used to facilitate the learning and development of their own self-awareness, self-management, relational skills and social awareness toward their responsible decision-making and professional success (Guerra, 2015). Problem-solving exchanges become snap-shot expressions that capture and demonstrate expressions of self. This allows teacher candidates to reflect and identify expressed patterns that may have otherwise been unnoticed. They learn to reflect not only on the solution but also on themselves as participants of the problem and more importantly the solution.

Future teacher preparation will need to address the unstated teacher candidate requisites of self-awareness to facilitate self-management. While social skills are usually assumed, this is not a valid assumption especially as teacher candidates enter a profession as graduates of abbreviated programs. If the teacher is to be monitoring their students' academic, behavioral, and social emotional learning, they should be provided the support to develop those skills in self as a social being, who will be working in a social and diverse setting.

BOOK ORIENTATION: ENGAGEMENT MANAGEMENT

Invitation. I was asked to speak to a group of student teachers, the meeting day arrived. I parked my car and entered an elementary school located within one of the poorest school districts in the city. It was a warm day and I was struck by the heat that I felt upon entering the school building. *I wondered <to myself> about the classroom temperatures for these children on the summer afternoons. Do they get drowsy from the heat?*

Event. I entered the small classroom to meet with the gathering of student teachers. Their demeanors were telling; things were not going well. The assigned meeting room was small and crowded. It appeared to be an early grade classroom. Small chairs filled the space as everyone closed in to find a seat. I barely had room to stand, my colleague introduced me and left. I smiled and asked how everyone was doing, only to receive weak smiles. I immediately began with a problem-solving activity to introduce the talk. I shared a stack of LIBRE Model problem-solving graphic organizer worksheets and explained the ground rules. The "LIBRE" acronym (and the Spanish word for free) used to stand for L-listen, I-identify a concern, B-brainstorm options, R-reality test next steps, and E-encourage to develop an action plan with timelines for accountability (Guerra, 2001, 2007, 2015).

Acknowledging the close surroundings, I asked that the student teachers offer each other the privacy for their own problem solving. Everyone agreed not to interfere with their neighbors' writing, and I promised to offer time and as much space as possible for each person to write down his/her thoughts and associated feelings. I explained that the problem-solving activity was intended for their own reflection and any action plans that they might want to develop. They were free to share their thoughts. However, I asked that they wait for the completion of the activity and our time together to do so. I teasingly asked for their affirmation that they would "keep their eyes on their own paper." They smiled, agreed and began.

Reflection. Thinking about what occurred next causes me great sadness. The student teachers listened to each cue and began to self-reflect as they responded to the LIBRE Model prompts. They allowed themselves to move into vulnerability and self-reflection. They wrote and cried. Tears ran down their cheeks. First, it was one student teacher, then the individual next to her, and then the next. Finally, one of the student teachers went to the corner cupboard, brought out a box of tissues, took one, and passed the box to another weeping student, who then passed the box to the next. The tissues were passed back and forth as I continued to present each of the problem-solving prompts.

While I never learned the specifics of what they each wrote on those sheets, I did speak to several student teachers after the event. One student teacher shared, "We never knew how overwhelming this job was going to be." As an educator, I listened closely. The student-teachers communicated great self-awareness and attentiveness to their new and foreign setting. This take-away still remains – teaching is more than a cognitive investment. There are emotional, social, and cultural demands in teaching that require attention, investment, and preparation.

Engagement management. Teacher preparation is more than a cognitive activity. Teachers are persons with lives which extend beyond the classroom. They have families, communities, and contexts that draw their attention in different directions. Thus, professional development, like any content or pedagogical development, involves investment in the self and social skills. Problem-solving is an ideal approach to address these levels and types of attentiveness and the LIBRE is an ideal venue. Problems draw the individual toward an increased attention from daily management to the challenge. Processing the problem-solving exchange with a LIBRE trained coach allows for the awareness of attention that is required. Attention to self-management is an important asset as a person becomes self-aware and begins to self-regulate. Attention, like content and pedagogy knowledge, facilitates the teacher's skilled agility to address challenges. We are preparing diverse professionals to work with the diverse needs of diverse individuals from diverse environments usually under a less than ideal setting, and often with limited financial, administrative or professional peer support. If we want to eliminate the "revolving door" of the teaching profession—teachers leaving the profession within the first five years—we need to address teaching as a "whole person experience." Social, emotional, cultural, and cognitive demands on *self* are equally important to successful professional development and these demands do not begin with teacher candidates' field experience. Rather, as persons, they are in constant transition. They begin as general students, moving forward into educator preparation programs. Then after much work and study, they assume the role of student teachers, excited and ready to apply all their skills. We need to prepare teacher candidates ahead of time so that they will be ready to face ongoing demands of change. Human development offers insight into the teacher candidates' roles and identities and experience.

Daughters and sons continue to grow and develop even before they leave their families for college with aspirations of becoming teachers. The big change occurs when they move into the larger university setting and away from the safety net that their home and family offer. They now are moving through various spheres and they experience a myriad of contexts, in some cases, extreme, as they move from one class to another. These different roles/identities and contexts carry their own associated demands. Students need to learn to be self-aware of these roles and identity changes so they can allocate attention to associated interpersonal demands. Students need the skills to become self-aware, strength-based problem-solvers so they are able to self-regulate and manage their engagement styles, which are identifiable through the initial and sustained attention within the LIBRE Model problem solving.

We will learn about the LIBRE Model four engagement styles, which are a combination of the *initial* and *sustained attention* defined as: *potential* (no initial and no sustained attention), *venting* (initial attention with no sustained attention), *goal-focused* (no initial attention with a sustained attention) and *actual engagement* (initial and sustained attention). The purpose is to address the teacher and the teacher's personal and professional development. The text follows two teacher candidates to examine their attention management and engagement observed through a series of problem-solving exchanges. Each teacher candidate is followed across multiple social contexts. While the two teacher candidates' paths were different in selected engagement styles, each achieved their engagement management to address the challenges with the resiliency observed in their investments, achievements, and success as teachers. The text examines each teacher candidate from a case study, multicultural, and action research lens. The expectation is that in addressing each teacher candidate from a different position, additional information can be uncovered.

The more skills that the teachers learn, the better that they will be in their new emerging role working within a diverse academic social setting. Their acquired social emotional learning skills will facilitate their resilience.

REFERENCES

CASEL. (1994). *Collaboration for academic, social, and emotional learning*. https://casel.org/about-2/

Guerra, N. S. (2001). *LIBRE Model*. Unpublished manuscript.

Guerra, N. (2007). LIBRE Model: Engagement styles in counseling. *Journal of Employment Counseling. 44*, 2–10.

Guerra, N. S. (2015). *Clinical problem-solving case management*. Rowan & Littlefield and Lexington Books.

INTRODUCTION

Creating a New Space

Headline and online global changes bombard the communication senses. Teachers, and those aspiring to be teachers, face external stimuli that entice and compromise their engagement, while they experience increased demands for their attention. This context can disorient the senses and derail the focus from setting intentional goals to making decisions-of-convenience. For instance, there is the student that wants to study but is compelled to listen to the closing day newscast. Distractive moments (intentionally, not from a judgmental perspective, but rather as any focus away from a defined goal) account for wasted time and investment. *Attention-distraction seesaws* heighten behavioral consequences and impact. Do I attend to what I know I must complete or attend to what is new or novel? The demands-on-time, combined with increasing distractibility, set the stage for potential personal and professional risk, not only for current teachers, but also for those students who aspire to one day be classroom teachers. Change is our guaranteed constant and the choices we make reflect our internal and external (self) dialogs.

Overview. Students enter teaching preparation programs with a noble cause— to make a difference in young persons' lives. Each receive training by skilled educators, yet, like returning young soldiers fresh from their first battlefield, some

---

Teacher Candidate Problem-Solving Engagement Styles:
LIBRE Model Self-Management Analysis, pages xiii–xx.
Copyright © 2022 by Information Age Publishing
www.infoagepub.com
All rights of reproduction in any form reserved.

xiii

encounter the overwhelming sensory experience that occurs with that first real "in class with real students" encounter. Sadly, many curricular approaches are taught as one-dimensional learning events. In other words, the content is taught in causal "if-then" terms. Teacher candidates are led to believe that if they present the content as learning, they will automatically be successful when they become teachers-of-record. There is little real understanding or anticipation about what is involved with working with real students, teachers, parents, the school environment, and administrators. What happened? How does the student experience attention-demand collide with attention-expectations? What about self-management? If there is way to support *self* within the midst of conflicting demands, what is it? How can one understand and prepare for the constant conflicting demands that occur as one moves from one context to another? The reality is that neither the teacher's academic experience nor the students themselves are one dimensional.[1]

Human agency involves facets of development and life experience (Bandura, 2001). Bronfenbrenner's ecological human development model (1979) describes this phenomenon as concentric circles in which persons grow and develop, not alone, but, rather within units, families, and systems. A notion that is extended to this inquiry, to consider what if the ecological systems that persons grow and develop within actually crossover and collide with emerging identified identities (Guerra et al., 2019)?

BOOK OUTLINE

Roles. Teacher preparation is more than a cognitive activity. Personally, and professionally, teachers have lives that extend beyond the classroom. They have families, communities, and contexts that draw their attention in different directions. These multi-roles require attention management grooming; like with any content or pedagogical skill, professional development involves learning. For the purpose of this work, problem-solving is a tool used to measure the teacher candidates' changes as they occurred over the course of their study. The foundational rationale of the problem-solving orientation is based on the nature of daily living. Problems occur; challenges draw increased attention and demand on the problem-solver (PS). The LIBRE Model problem-solving template provided consistent cues to facilitate the PSs' internal and externally expressed thoughts as they moved from the comfort of daily management to attend to identified challenge; their expressed attention resulted in varying engagement styles and resolution outcomes (Guerra, 2001). Attention, as a construct, was found to be a critical component of the problem-solving exchange.

Problem-solving and self-management skills facilitate cognitive change; however, to become a proficient teacher, there are other requirements, including social management skills, which offer teacher candidates a classroom management tool. We are preparing diverse professionals to work with diverse needs, under

---

[1] Note: The research reported was supported in part by a Federally-funded Title V grant

less-than-ideal settings, and often with limited financial support. If we want to eliminate the teaching profession "revolving door," with teachers leaving the profession within the first five years, we need to address teaching as a "whole person experience." Social, emotional, cultural, and cognitive demands on *self* are as important to successful professional development as pedagogy. Transitions do not begin with the students' field experience. Rather, students are in constant transition. They begin as students, and segue into student teacher roles, and eventually to become teachers. Human development offers insight to the multiple roles and identities student teachers experience.

Context. Students move through various systems as they experience a myriad of contexts. These multiple environmental settings carry associated demands. Self-awareness of these environments bring associated interpersonal demands and changes; attention must be allocated to these external demands. Students need skills to facilitate self-awareness; strength-based problem-solvers can self-regulate and manage their engagement styles, defined in initial and sustained attention, across contexts (Guerra, 2007).

LIBRE Model. The LIBRE Model is a problem-solving activity; the acronym for L-listen, I-identify a problem, B-brainstorm resolution options, R-reality test, E-encourage, is used to identify problem-solvers responses (Guerra, 2001; 2009). The problem-solver creates the problem-solving record. The problem-solver's words are tracked. With this research study, teacher candidates were provided the LIBRE Model prompts by a trained LIBRE Model facilitator who held a master's degree as a counselor and functioned as a transitional coach. The series of problem-solving exchanges become a supportive, reflective resource and reference to address challenges that the teachers experienced. The identified "attention demands," context, and associated response patterns, engagement styles, were collected with each problem-solving exchange each semester. The transitional coach/facilitator and teacher candidate worked together to examine the problem-solving language and resolution effectiveness. The coach tracked the teacher candidate's attention pattern. S/he accumulated group data (the accumulated individual problem-solving events) and evaluated the participant's progress, intersectionality of role, context, and resiliency in whole person development. To begin key components of the LIBRE Model concept are provided.

Attention. Problem-solver attention can be identified in LIBRE Model problem-solving exchange. Discrete attention patterns emerge as the problem-solver dissects and explores the problem. ***Initial Attention*** is defined as language-investment in problem-oriented social context, brainstorming, and reality-testing of generated options. ***Sustained attention*** is defined as the respondents' continued investment to focus on an identified challenge up to the development of a resolution. Together, Initial and Sustained attention patterns combine to assess engagement styles (Guerra, 2009). The problem-solver's responses to the LIBRE Model prompts are the data used to monitor attention changes. Once the problem-solver identifies a focal problem (goal), the remainder of the exchange shifts to processing of that challenge. Brainstorming and reality-testing occur, culminating with the development of a resolution. The individual's allocated attention over the course of the entire exchange is then assessed to categorize engagement styles (Guerra, 2009).

Engagement Styles. The resultant four identified engagement styles represent differential attentiveness preferences; they are not traits, rather they are learned patterns to process attention demands. While individuals are not restricted to engage in one engagement style of attentiveness over another, dominant styles are commonplace. Once these styles are identified, the facilitator and teacher explore self-awareness possibilities for managing attention. Individuals that are less attentive or non-attentive have compromised problem-solving success and often end up revisiting challenges to consider another possible outcome (Guerra, 2001, 2007, 2015).

The LIBRE Model identifies non-engagement as *potential engagement*, primarily because it is assumed the individual has the capability to engage, however, for some unknown reason, the person has selected not to engage. The LIBRE Model also identifies patterns of engagement and non-engagement. These can be seen as styles ranging from engaged to partial engagement to non-engaged. The individuals' passive attentive engagement style is characterized in the individual who selects to use avoidant problem-solving strategies. Their expressed language suggests they do not have any problems, or they are ignoring the problem; therefore, they do not need to invest.

The opposite of passive attentive engagement is an active attentive style, identified as *actual engagement.* This style is observed in the individuals' whose problem-solving language involves detailed and specific exploration of options and resolutions. A variation of the highly invested person is an individual who exhibits a shorter attentive investment, defined as a *venting engagement.* This person's observed investment is initially detailed. The problem-solver's invested language suggests a commitment to the challenge that is described in detail; however, once the problem is described, limited investment is offered, and no resolution is sought. This problem-solver offers detailed problem descriptions by repeating the concern with no resolution interest. The final engagement style preference is identified as *goal-focused.* This problem-solver is solution-oriented; there is no interest in addressing the problem context. The problem-solver wants only to address the focal challenge; this single problem, without interest in exploring context, is the problem-solver's sole attention and investment with the purpose of developing a resolution.

Over this five-year period of study, some teacher candidate participants transitioned from engaged to more focused engagement; non-engagement to engagement, engagement to non-engagement, and others who selected to remain engaged with their one defined style. Others opted out of the program and/or university as non-engaged. Finally, there were those who were comfortable with their evolving self-awareness, management, and engagement style explorations.

The involved researchers recorded the teacher candidates' engagement usage over the transitioning period to reflect with each their growth and development into their teaching professions.

The LIBRE Model, APA Multicultural Model, and action research framework were used for the overall discussion. This systemic presentation provides a center piece to the discussion of growth, self-awareness (roles), self-management (within context), and change (resiliency and growth). The LIBRE Model (Guerra, 2001), problem-solving tool, captures and records the teacher candidates' internal and external thinking. The action research structure highlights the community-of-self, internal and external dialog and the Multicultural Model addresses the complexity of movement from one context to another.

THEORETICAL FRAMEWORK

There is a personal psychosocial-cognitive learning experience involved in teacher career professional development (Guerra et al., 2019). Engagement style awareness is observed in personal and professional self-managed attentiveness. Jon, an experienced teacher, explained, "I move across all four engagement styles each day. In the morning, as I listen to the day's announcements, I am *potential*. Then, moving into my classroom, I become *goal-focused* as I present the daily lesson. By lunch, I join my fellow teachers in the lunchroom to *vent*. At the end of the day, I am *actual* (actively) engaged as I assess what went well and what will need to be revisited tomorrow." As educators, we recognize the importance of attentiveness linked to teaching and classroom management. We acknowledge the importance of engagement as associated with behavior and the learning experience; however, the monitoring of attention (self and others), while acknowledged, is often assumed without any mechanisms to gauge or monitor (Guerra, 2009b). Self-awareness facilitates self-regulation and self-management (Bradberry & Greaves, 2009).

For teachers holding a primary role in facilitating the learning experience, proactive attentive engagement style awareness toward their students and self is critical. More fundamental, is the value in providing teachers-in-training the resources to manage their engagement and the engagement of their students. Preliminary findings suggest that personal-awareness and attention management proficiency exponentially facilitated student monitoring and classroom management, as well as resiliency (Guerra, 2007).

Personal (attention) awareness facilitates personal management (Bradberry & Greaves, 2009). Filtering attention becomes automatic as a person matures and adapts to individual culture, learned experiences, and conscious means for receiving and processing the ongoing flow of information (Guerra et al., 2018). Alvarez and Cavanagh (2004) depict attention routines as consciously initiated action by setting a goal toward a reportable outcome. Strategic automaticity facilitates action control and the implementation of intentions. Gollwitzer and Sheeran (2006) suggest that intentional automaticity may facilitate attention management. Carol

Dweck's (2016) work describes this as a mindset, which she asserts, "the view you adopt for yourself profoundly affects the way you lead your life" (p. 6). Cialdini (2007) asserts that automaticity is the shortcut used to manage our complex world filled with stimulating demands. Referring back to Jon, the experienced teacher, he selected to engage differently at key points of the day. He strategically engaged with automaticity as the school day cycle progressed. In the morning, announcements cued him to assume a passive (*Potential*) engagement, he became *Goal-focused* in his classroom as he taught his students. He made sure to communicate each objective of the lesson. Moving to lunch, he was free to *Vent* in the teacher's lounge with the rest of his peers and by the close of the day, his final transition was to an *Actual* engagement; his opportunity to evaluate and plan for the next day. Weiber and Sassenberg (2006) examined automaticity of implementation intention to assert that "implementation intentions lead to attention attraction effects for their corresponding situational cues, above and beyond goal intentions" (p. 744). They found that when their participants formed an *implementation intention* toward their attention, they were better able to maintain that attention.

This observation of self-awareness, and strategic self-managed—*initial* and *sustained attention*—found in problem solving over the course of a school day, offers much to the notion of growth and professional development. For example, a problem-solver who is willing to identify a problem, but not invest in developing a resolution, will likely not find change or resolution; not because it is not there, rather, because there is not attention to this level of investment. The problem-solver willing to identify a problem, formulate a goal intention, and develop a plan will more willingly commit to its execution. Attention and where the attentions are allocated impact function. Weiber and Sassenberg concluded, "automatic attention effects seem to be an integral part of successful action control through implementation intentions" (p. 748). Attentiveness plays a role in action/non-action investment and management. Thus, the intention is to explore attention, as presented in problem solving, with two teacher candidates working through an accelerated masters' degree with teacher certification requirement embedded.

BOOK ORGANIZATION

Section 1 (Chapters 1–4) addresses instrumentation. Chapter 1 examines individuals' *attention awareness* expressed in attractions and distractions. This is the lens used to examine individual engagement. Weiber and Sassenberg (2006) explain that it is difficult to disengage from implemented attention. Once one is on a path, there are expressed commitments; there are levels of automaticity, and the comfort of investments, that tie the individual to that expressed path. Attention is examined as it appears in problem solving. Chapter 2 presents the LIBRE Model problem solving and data collection protocol. Using the LIBRE Problem-Solving Model: through L-listen, I-identify, B-brainstorm, R-reality-test, and E-encourage, (LIBRE) (Guerra, 2009a), attention is presented within the theoretical context of social cognitive and goal management. Problem-solving *Initial* and *Sustained At-*

tention are discussed. Chapter 3 addresses engagement styles as investments in *Initial* and S*ustained Attention*. Four engagement styles are presented and the implications of each are discussed (Guerra, 2009b). Chapter 4 addresses the APA Multicultural Model as a context to frame the case study analysis.

Section 2 Research plan and distinct lens presentations are applied to the case study sample (Chapters 5, 6, and 7). Chapter 5 addresses the overall research plan. The two teacher candidates' narratives are examined as case studies. Chapter 6 is the case study of a Hispanic female teacher candidate; identified with action-oriented attentiveness patterns that fluctuated to support her incremental change. Chapter 7 is the case study of a Hispanic male teacher candidate who was observed changing from non-engagement to focused engagement to non-engagement reflections, ultimately completing the program to begin his career as a teacher. In each case, the engagement style awareness and management facilitated their unique transition into the teaching career.

Section 3 addresses the multi-facets of the teacher candidate experience. The APA Multicultural Model and action research structures are applied to the two case studies (Chapters 8–9). Chapter 8 addresses the two-problem-solving case studies and the participant changes expressed in context and engagement through the APA Multicultural Guidelines ecological model lens. Implications of personal and professional challenge management are discussed. Clauss-Ehler et al.'s (2019) APA Multicultural Guidelines facilitate the discussion of an ecological approach to context, identity, and intersectionality. Chapter 9 examines the expressed *attention* patterns, engagement styles. The action research framework highlights the individual as a community, *community-of-self* to explore the internal dialogs of culture, community participation and evaluate effective solutions. This structure allows insight into the daily self-as-community challenges and offers a view of attention as presented within transformational self-awareness, a community-of-one, where context, challenge, and attention differ one from the other. Chapter 10 concludes with a summary and discussion of intersectionality, attention to *self, self-as-group,* and *self-awareness* in problem-solving toward *self-management;* skills that have the potential of impacting professional success and resiliency in *social-management,* as well as, contributing to an overall growth and intersectionality development.

REFERENCES

Alvarez, G. A., & Cavanagh, P. (2004). The capacity of visual short-term memory is set both by visual information load and by number of objects. *Psychological Science, 15*(2), 106–111.

Bandura, A. (2001). Social cognitive theory: An agentic perspective. *Annual Review of Psychology, 52,* 1–26.

Bradberry, T., & Greaves, J. (2009). *Emotional intelligence 2.0.* TalentSmart.

Bronfenbrenner. (1979). *The ecology of human development: Experiments by nature and design.* Harvard Press.

Cialdini, R. B. (2007). *The psychology of influence of persuasion.* Collins Business Essentials.

Clauss-Ehlers, C. S., Chiriboga, D. A., Hunter, S., Roysircar, G., Tummala-Narra, Pratyusha, K., & Kazak, A. E. (2019). APA Multicultural guidelines executive summary: Ecological approach to context, identity, and intersectionality. *American Psychologist, 74*(2), 232–244.

Dweck, C. (2016). *Mindset the new psychology of success.* Ballantine Books.

Gollwitzer, P. M., & Sheeran, P. (2006). Implementation intentions and goal achievement: A meta-analysis of effect and processes. *Advances in Experimental Social Psychology, 33,* 69–119.

Guerra, N. S. (2001). *LIBRE Model.* Unpublished manuscript.

Guerra, N. S. (2007). LIBRE Model: Engagement styles in counseling. *Journal of Employment Counseling, 44,* 2–10.

Guerra, N. S. (2009). LIBRE stick figure tool: A graphic organizer to foster self-regulated social cognitive problem solving. *Interventions in Schools and Clinics, 44*(4), 229–233.

Guerra, N. S. (2009a). LIBRE Model stick figure tool: Graphic organizer. *Interventions in Schools and Clinics, 44*(4), 1–5.

Guerra, N. S. (2009b). Illustrations of engagement styles: Four teacher candidates. *Teacher Education and Practice, 22*(1), 95–117.

Guerra, N. S. (2015). *Clinical problem solving: Case management.* Rowman & Littlefield.

Guerra, N. S., Carrillo, C., & Hernandez, A. E. (2019). Latina experience in higher education: Problem-solving to facilitate student success. *Journal of Creativity in Mental Health, 14*(4), 406–423.

Weiber, F., & Sassenberg, K. (2006). I can't take my eyes off of it—Attention attraction effects of implementation intentions. *Social Cognition, 24*(6), 723–752.

SECTION 1

IDENTITY FACETS WITHIN PROBLEM-SOLVING ENGAGEMENT STYLES

CHAPTER 1

ATTENTION: WHEN, WHERE, AND WHY

The Construct of Attention

Maslow described attention as investment to meet a need. For example, a hungry man will attend to seeking food to meet that need. Attention is allocated for a purpose. Extending Maslow's analogy, if the basic need is met, attention will be extended to "felt security, love, confidence" (Kaufman, 2020). In application, there are a combination of internal and external attentiveness decisions that are then behaviorally observable in "playful, less inhibited, smiling and social<ability>." As the individual attends, receives the met need, learned responses (as described above) occur. Bandura describes vicarious learning as attention to unintentional learning events that occurs as one observes others. Perhaps this person learned to smile in response to receiving the food he sought. Thus, attention is ongoing; when, where, why, and how attention is managed results in change that in social context impacts not only the person but those in community.

Attention—When. Let's consider the influencing features involved in the decision to go to college or become a college student. Students' attend to interests in deciding on career paths. Perhaps influenced externally by who they trust, how they were raised, who they valued, culture, experiences, and affordances provid-

Teacher Candidate Problem-Solving Engagement Styles:
LIBRE Model Self-Management Analysis, pages 3–9.
Copyright © 2022 by Information Age Publishing
www.infoagepub.com
All rights of reproduction in any form reserved.

4 • TEACHER CANDIDATE PROBLEM-SOLVING ENGAGEMENT STYLES

ed. Internally, the personal goals that they have attended to for themselves are theirs alone. Often, they have learned to process and best navigate the different social contexts. The immediacy of these decisions come into full force as they encounter pressure to maximize their attention to goals and/or success; in this case the desire to become a teacher. Human development and developmental theorists have much to offer in examining college student attentiveness as behavioral patterns in relation to self, context, and the flow of data associated with what they intend to weigh in on and attend to.

Identity. Erikson (1968) describes this phase in life within his psychosocial model as, *Intimacy and Solidarity versus Isolation*. He explains that all individuals process life- long ego concerns with marked crisis points. Age-stage climaxes demand responses that set forth positive or negative trajectory developmental paths. The adolescent emerging from Stage 5: *Identity and Repudiation versus Identity Diffusion* occurs in or during high school. The incoming freshman student has likely experienced this *identity* ego crisis and resolved it with either a positive or negative orientation.

Depending on the attentiveness to events and resolution of those experiences, Stage 5 *Identity*, s/he enters college with some identity configuration that aligns with self as defined by the student role. Social considerations such as "fitting-in" and not standing out as someone who does not belong at the university may be a focus of attention for these traditional-aged incoming students. Theoretically, the college student is seeking a true self. Erikson suggests this is a time to find *self* through affiliations with others. Each student faces the management of identity and attention demands that accompany this crisis point, in addition to managing the new academic environment. Managing new experiences requires resilience, which develops from protective factors, sometimes referred to as environmental supports (Clauss-Ehlers, 2004).

Attention—Where. The college students' attention oriented to prior experiences offers advantages that can be characterized as assets or affordances. These affordances offer additional opportunities. Thus, the more affordances, the more opportunities. The accumulation of these acquired skills sets the stage for the college students and likely will influence where they attend.

Affordances. Gibson and Pick (2000) explain the artifact of *affordances* as the relationship between the persons and their environments. For example, more privileged students will likely have the advantage of *affordances* such as educated families and mentors or coaches who prepare them for college. They experience supportive freedoms that assist in their understanding of academic expectations; what to attend to and the importance of developing know-how strategies from their prior academic experiences and affiliations. First-generation or minority students from families with limited educational backgrounds may receive incomplete academic background support and their affordances offer a different picture. While on one hand, there is a similar dream of what could be, the difference is that the desired destination comes without a roadmap for the student with limited experience. What to attend to and how to attend to the academic expectations are not defined for the student who has never had these preparatory experiences.

To expand this analogy, consider two students: one student with multiple affordances, a car with gas, representing a privileged background and educational support; to another student with fewer affordances, does not have a car or gas yet is expected to drive and arrive at the same destination at the same time. Self-efficacy develops through affordances, the student with opportunity and experience is secure of self in this familiar setting. The student without the diverse affordances is struggling with what to attend to and how. Thus, affordances are critical in managing the many unknowns that accompany the higher education experience.

Not only is background a factor, *identity* is also a feature impacting students' higher education experiences. Students' *affordances* facilitate the attention required to manage skill development. Attentiveness involves both self-awareness and self-management; handling complex, unscripted demands requires skills. Questions arise: What skills can educators teach to facilitate attention management? What skills can assist students in developing focused attention to a desired goal? How does attention link to engagement? What happens when students' affordances differ from those traditionally associated with university success?

The new college experience is also a fresh *context*; how students see and attend to the university must be considered a relation to the many distinct prior lenses. Depending upon their societal advantages, affordances, experiences, and met needs, students will ascribe to different attention needs in meeting academic expectations, while balancing personal needs and experiences. Thus, initial and sustaining attention is needed to reach the person's ultimate identified goal, stated as the focal problem. For example, the goal of acquiring a degree. Depending upon who the student is, background context, focus and goal may differ, in addition to the skills required to meet the need.

For students with educated parents, the higher education experience is socially known; they are ready to seek higher order esteem and affirmation with this more familiar setting and experience. These students' attention is likely to be more directed toward learning and personal efficacy found in meeting the academic challenge. For minority students of less-educated parents, the academic advantage may not be in place. Their first attention, investment, is oriented toward safety and finding a "fit" in this unknown setting. Hierarchically, peer social exchanges are more important than classroom learning, which is secondary to social identity and social development.

Automaticity. Cialdini (2007) asserts that attention and the influences of persuasion can be described in terms of *automaticity*. Imagine for a moment encountering a barrage of stimuli, and the automatic sorting that occurs as you respond to one stimulus and not others. The constant flow of stimuli sets the stage for an *attention-distraction seesaw*, where competing demand-responses arise. For example, a student wants to invest in attending a social event to better fit into the

6 • TEACHER CANDIDATE PROBLEM-SOLVING ENGAGEMENT STYLES

college experience. However, her family has a gathering that they expect her to attend at the same time.

The intersection of unconscious, subconscious, conscious attention, values, culture, and societal customs are factors that contribute to established preferences, and to the struggle in creating new customs. Given the person's background, race, ethnicity, social class, gender, and identity, the child develops from adolescence to young adulthood. These personalized beliefs, cultures, and values facilitate response decisions. When confronted with what and how to attend, there is a greater likelihood that the student will attend to the more familiar and/or valued stimuli with the more familiar behavioral autonomous responses. Similarly, the student will assign lesser attention to less valued stimuli.

The individual establishes "attention demand" categorized responses that are then used to manage internalized attention preferences that have been developing since birth. These attention patterns are often presented as cultural values. For example, a student grows up in a nurturing community that values helping one-another. When the student reaches the higher education campus, s/he begins actively seeking like-minded students. This student is drawn to and seeks individuals with similar identities, cultural values, and affordances. Automatic sorting occurs as the student orients self to this new setting. The familiarity of the stimuli matches to the automatic response. Why? This automatic allocation of attention allows the individual the cognitive space needed to attend to unfamiliar or novel response-demands. Stimuli of greater interest or perceived greater consequence will demand attention.

Attention—Why. Culture, language, race, and ethnicity influence the attention given to specific content. Cialdini's research, with cults and advertising, provides a strong case for the passive influencing features associated with persuasive management and the attention awarded to novelty or social mores. Cialdini explains with the cult member who offers a flower to elicit an automatic response. The attentiveness sought is to exchange something in return, quid pro quo. Something tangible is offered with the expectation that something will be reciprocated. In this case, the attention of the person receiving the flower addresses novelty/curiosity to heighten attention. The recipient in return has an implied expectation to listen to the cult person's invitation to join. In addition, of interest with this particular example is the notion of senses involved; the sight, smell, and hearing. Each are socially linked to automatic favorable response.

Self-actualization. Maslow's (1943) hierarchy of needs provides a parallel picture of how individuals manage attention. He asserts that all individuals are motivated to become self-actualized. Displayed as a pyramid (a description that he did not develop), the base represents physiological needs that must be met prior to progressing forward to seek safety. Once individuals meet base needs, they are motivated to seek social needs. Subsequently, individuals seek esteem after meeting social needs. The ultimate self-actualization point is represented as the peak of the pyramid. Maslow describes this acquired goal as both the most altruistic and self-aware pivotal point for maximum potential.

According to Maslow, a healthy individual is fluid in their growth and response to adversity—"we can learn from self-actualizing people what the ideal attitude toward work might be under the most favorable circumstances. These highly evolved individuals assimilate their work into the self, i.e., work actually becomes part of the self, part of the individual's definition of himself" (Maslow, 1998, p. 1). Maslow's presentation not only provides a picture of a person in the workplace, but also of a student preparing for a career.

Kaufman (2020) explains that it was not Maslow's intention to frame self-actualization as the ultimate progression in his theory rather he had planned on presenting multiple needs occurring simultaneously; the idea was to introduce movement, growth, and development allowing for transcendence. We are best of ourselves as we intersect, merge and meld with the best-selves to contribute to the betterment of the larger community. This growth-in-movement adds to the discussion of what to attend to, why, and how. Growth occurs with movement, affordances, and awareness. Attention to these larger and different settings, draw attention. The individual that becomes aware of the new context experiences a change and potential challenge; to have an internal (contextual systems as community-of-self influences to make sense of the new setting) dialog or to ignore the unfamiliar and not invest. The decision making and selected investment contributes to the selected/preferred engagement styles.

Attention as a Construct. Attention develops with awareness and self-management. Personal need has an automaticity of efficiency to allow for attention capacity to be available for addressing unfamiliar and items of curiosity. Individuals attend to social exchanges. Until they develop skills to allow for the automaticity involved in holding appropriate attention to social exchanges, they will likely direct attention to more basic needs, such as how best to fit in. As individuals develop skills, they attend to context and environmental demands from a self-actualized awareness and adjust attention as social context demands; it is here that differences occur depending on the role assumed and that role-in-context. For example, the student who is a mother and a student. She is a student in the school context; at home she is the mother. Kaufman (2020) explains that Maslow had one ultimate hierarchical need described as "the best in us meld with the best in others and the world around us," this transcendence allows for attention to the greater good in all for the greater good of all.

REALITIES FACING HIGHER EDUCATION

Zweig (2008) explains that there are three major class distinctions found in the United States and higher education systems. These defined classes are based upon power, independence in decision-making and quality of life. Additionally, these class differences account for capitalists' power and dominance in the workplace and political arena; with these persons holding the responsibility for the largest

8 • TEACHER CANDIDATE PROBLEM-SOLVING ENGAGEMENT STYLES

corporations and control not only their own money, but also the nation's wealth. Zweig asserts that this dominance of white males in top political positions defines the "ruling class" within the United States (2008).

Meanwhile, as the middle-class continues to lose power, there are those who speculate that the working class will one day generate the same salary income of the middle class without the associated respect and independence in decision-making (Zweig, 2008). As we consider individuals of privilege versus first generation students, a less than ideal pipeline is predicted. In the current 25-year-old age group, 80.4% graduated from high school; however, only 24.4% went on to achieve either a bachelor's degree or a higher professional degree (Vespa et al., 2013). DeNavas-Walt and Proctor (2015) report that approximately 47 million people within the United States live in poverty, with the non-Hispanic White making up 10.1%, Asians 12%, Hispanics 23.6%, and African Americans 26.2%.

In 2011, examining the frequency of poor children in the United States, 19% were White Anglo-Saxon children living below the poverty line compared to 37% African American and 34% Hispanic American (DeNavas-Walt et al., 2013). This suggests that not only are minority children growing up in poverty, but non-minority, white children, while in smaller percentages, are also being impacted by the societal and political climate. If this trend continues, higher education and the students who will be offered the opportunity to attend will look very different. The needs and experiences of those future students will also come with unique motivational needs and attention experiences, leading to different learning curve experiences. Yet, these investments have the potential for a positive return as only 5% of the poverty level is made up of individuals who have at least a bachelor's degree (DeNavas-Walt & Proctor, 2015). Education is the variable to create change; however, the complexity in recruitment will need to match with specificity in supportive retention efforts.

Take Away Considerations. The complexity of this attention investment can be disorienting for any student. For the less focused or experienced student, it can be overwhelming. For the first-generation and/ or minority students' attentiveness, the sustaining attentiveness may be directed to physiological needs. Maslow clearly states, survival/safety is foundational before pursuing belonging or affiliation. Returning here to the privileged student with a history of affordances and all basic needs met, the privileged student's attention is to seek opportunity. Physiological needs have long been established and the security of a credit card, cash at hand, and family ready to assist, motivate the student to attend to learning and exploring new affiliations. The growing reality, however, is that students entering the class may not be ready to attend. Multiple needs and multiple challenges may frame their participation and investment.

In summary, there is value in exploring what students attend to and how they attend. Identity and the affordances that individuals experience contribute to their views and their development. Automaticity facilitates where and what students attend to, even as they move forward toward self-actualization. The challenge is that at times automaticity is the preference to remain efficient. As Bandura (2006) reports, all are agents for their own life. Context, culture, and experience are important considerations in addressing the student higher education experience. Self-actualization involves attention; how attention is managed, and where it is offered. Our goal with this discussion is to address attention and investment in engagement styles as an opportunity to move away from automaticity.

REFERENCES

Bandura, A. (2006). Toward a psychology of human agency. *Perspectives on Psychological Science, 1*(2), 164–180.

Cialdini, R. B. (2007). *Influence: The psychology of persuasion.* Collins Business Essential.

Clauss-Ehlers, C. S. (2004). Re-inventing resilience: A model of culturally-focused resilient adaptation. In C. S. Clauss-Ehlers & M. D. Weist (Eds.), *Community planning to foster resilience in children* (pp. 27–41). Kluwer.

DeNavas-Walt, C., & Proctor, B. D. (2015). Income and poverty in the United States: 2014. *Current Reports* (pp. 60–252). U.S. Census Bureau. U.S. Government Printing Office.

DeNavas-Walt, C., Proctor, B. D., & Smith, J. C. (2013). Income, poverty, and health insurance coverage in the United States: 2012. *Current population reports* (pp. 60–245). U.S. Census Bureau.

Erikson, E. H. (1968). *Identity: Youth and crisis.* Norton.

Gibson, E. J., & Pick, A. D. (2000). *An ecological approach to perceptual learning and development.* Oxford University Press.

Kaufman, S. B. (2020). *Transcend: The new science of self-actualization.* TarcherPerigee.

Maslow, A. H. (1943). A theory of human motivation. *Psychological Review, 50*(4), 370–396.

Maslow, A. H. (1998). *Maslow on management.* John Wiley & Sons, Inc.

Vespa, J., Lewis, J. M., & Kreider, R. M. (2013). *America's families and living arrangements: 2012, Current population reports* (pp. 20–570). U.S. Census Bureau.

Zweig, M. (2008). What's class got to do with it? In K. E. Rosenblum & T. C. Travis (Eds.), *The meaning of difference: American constructions of race, sex and gender, social class, sexual orientation, and disability* (5th ed., pp. 81–87). MacGraw-Hill.

CHAPTER 2

THE LIBRE PROBLEM-SOLVING MODEL CONCEPTUALIZED

There is comfort in the familiar; no one actively goes about seeking problems. Problems are more often experienced as an unwelcome guest. Similarly, there is confidence in knowing how things work; there is gained efficacy in knowing how to work through familiar challenges. For example, your car needs gas. The solution is just around the corner at the local gas station; pull out your card and fill up the tank. There is a security in repeating the same behaviors to receive the same return; thoughts, and actions with impact as one anticipates the familiar resulting outcomes. These well-worn patterns allow for the freedom to attend to other novelty or interest areas. If only personal growth could be an ideal place to take comfort, where needs are met as they arise. Maslow describes the opposite side of growth as deficiency need; a D-realm motivated by a lack of need (Kaufman, 2020). Unfortunately, life includes challenges. Self-managed attention to a singular problem (or need) introduces the potential for change and/or an alternate path leading to an alternate outcome. Problem-solving becomes important; being able to successfully overcome an obstacle assists with resiliency. And the position assumed as one enters the problem-solving exchange has equal weight to the decisions assumed.

Teacher Candidate Problem-Solving Engagement Styles:
LIBRE Model Self-Management Analysis, pages 11–19.
Copyright © 2022 by Information Age Publishing
www.infoagepub.com
All rights of reproduction in any form reserved.

12 • TEACHER CANDIDATE PROBLEM-SOLVING ENGAGEMENT STYLES

LIBRE Model. The LIBRE problem-solving Model was developed to encourage a creative, strength-based, positive approach to identifiable challenges (Guerra, 2009). And before introducing this problem-solving approach, I'd like to share the Model's inception. A group of clergy, social workers, nurses, and counselors, all educated mental health professionals, came together, gathered with a noble cause. The goal was to help the public low-income housing residents address challenges associated with limited education, minimal skills, and the economic vulnerability that defined them. While these trained professionals were excited to begin this honorable project, they quickly realized that their shared goal had created a new problem. Each had been professionally trained to orient to distinct facets of the at-risk challenge. As they listened to each other, they realized the diversity in their professional training and experiences had created a new obstacle. They stopped; I received an invitation to intervene. I listened to my colleagues and agreed to assist. It was from this encounter that I developed The LIBRE Model—Listen –Identify the focal problem—Brainstorm options—Reality test—Encourage.

I used an acronym for the Spanish word free, "L-I-B-R-E" to highlight the model's strength-based approach. The goal was to create a common language for a shared curriculum. The **L-listen and list** prompt addresses environmental challenges and **I-identify a specific problem** is used to hone-in upon a single challenge. As I met with the group, I thanked them for the opportunity to assist, restating the L-I-B-R-E framework. We continued with the restatement of Listen<ing> and I-identify<ing> the challenge. Each prompt was presented, allowing time for all to speak. Their well-articulated problem was stated as: "How are we going to address the needs of these public housing individuals?" The question became the shared goal for the remainder of the session. Next, I offered the **B-brainstorm** prompt. We considered, evaluated, and prioritized multiple options. We reviewed the prioritized list before moving forward to the **R-reality testing** prompt. We explored the implications and behavioral investments that accompanied each option.

Up to this point in this process, the LIBRE Model appears to be a traditional problem-solving model. However, I intentionally framed the problem-solving process as a reflection to acknowledge where they have been and are now, with the encouragement to consider an action plan to explore change. I wanted to **E-encourage** the problem-solver(s) (PS) to consider resolution development. Encouragement is essential, as it affirms the individual strengths, willingness to process possibilities and acknowledges the possibilities of change. The Encourage prompt facilitates continued investment and includes accountability toward the development of a resolution action plan. From its inception, the LIBRE Model engagement is to orient investment toward attention to change (Guerra, 2001) and the result of this community investment was their professional shared plan. The group's common problem-solving language and facilitated steps provided them the security and comfort to attend to their unique skilled services. They developed their plans and coordinated in a fashion that allowed all participants to fashion their service to their unique training, and skilled contributions.

This public housing community supported problem-solving as a benefit. They knew their need and what they wanted; this created value to their investment and secured their use of professional training. The strength-based problem-solving exchange affirmed the PS; even if they would not have left with a solution, they would have walked away valued and respected.

What is the LIBRE Model? The strength-based LIBRE Model is a problem-solving activity. The acronym "LIBRE" organizes and frames the problem-solving exchange. The LIBRE Model reflects a metacognitive exchange. Five L-I-B-R-E prompts guide the problem-solving process. The LIBRE Model provides the PS a series of scripted prompts. The facilitator offers the prompts and records the PS's responses. At a global level, the problem-solving provides a glimpse into the internal thinking of the PS. The PS and facilitator establish a relationship of trust, confidence, and respect. The PS is secure in this self-exploration.

Theoretical Underpinning. Problem-solving is a basic mode for organizing knowledge. If we consider what is known from an observable unknown, we have in essence defined a problem (e.g., Duda & Shortliffe, 1983; Larkin et al., 1980). The detail, specificity and coherence in thought, and investment provided as information to address the problem becomes context for the problem-solving attentiveness that is observed from the beginning of the problem-solving exchange, up to the development of resolution plan (Guerra, 2015). The PS is responsible for managing the problem-solving responses, organization, and presentation. The LIBRE Model includes a PS, and problem-solving facilitator to assist; the PS has the freedom and platform to speak of all thoughts without judgment, while the facilitator records the responses.

How it works. The multi-faceted problem-solving activity requires a PS's attention. The PS is invited to self-reflect, to identify a goal (the identified problem stated as a question) and to brainstorm with sub-skills that include: the management of realistic and unrealistic options, and to implement abstract thinking as skills related to reality testing. The depth of exploration, of plausible resolution, and implications are all up to the PS.

Recorded Responses. Only the PS's responses are recorded; the verbatim record is documented onto the LIBRE Model Stick Figure (LMSF), a graphic organizer that provides a visual to the PS (and facilitator) as they progress through the activity (Guerra, 2009, 2015). The stick figure graphic provides: (1) a user-friendly visual; similar to a black-lined coloring book drawing, the LMSF is a stick figure drawing with open space for the PS to contemplate, and (2) is a simplified representation of how a problem impacts the PS. The implied picture is provided, the common characterization of a stressed person with the person's hair standing on end, the PS is given space to address—what makes their hair stand on end? The drawing continues, as the problem weight continues for the person holding the problem; it is captured within the rectangular box. The intention with placing the

14 • TEACHER CANDIDATE PROBLEM-SOLVING ENGAGEMENT STYLES

problem on the shoulders is to imply the slumping down burden, the beaten-down feeling as the PS carries the problem on the shoulders, as the problem grows. As that problem remains unaddressed, it may cause mid-body discomfort, sleeplessness wrestling with the problem, perhaps even a stomachache. Thus, the midriff provides spaces for brainstorming and reality-testing. This graphic area is to address the processing of the problem. To the point of decision, the feet represent that forward movement in action, the processing of action plans developed or not; this encouragement is designed to acknowledge any problem-solving investment.

LIBRE Model Illustrated. Jan is a first-generation undergraduate student who has been selected to become a PS. She is invited to freely address challenges and bothersome thoughts that she has experienced over the last several weeks. **First:** the LIBRE Model ground rules are presented as "working principles" that define the parameters of the problem-solving exchange, see Table 2.1. LIBRE Model Ground Rules. The ground rules address the problem-solving management of *Confidentiality,* with the only breach occurring if she addresses issues of harm to "self" or others. Should she speak of plans to injure self or others, these thoughts/ actions are reportable. *Safety* is important along with autonomy, the development of *Independence* and problem-solving *self-efficacy*. The facilitator answers all of the questions about the exchange before offering the first prompt. **Second:** Once Jan understands the ground rules and the LIBRE Model steps, she indicates that she is ready, and the problem-solving exchange begins.

L—Listen and List challenges—introduces an open space for the PS to begin tapping into self. Her thoughts, feelings, and attention are drawn to the environmental context. The facilitator begins, "Let's talk about what is going on right now. I will list everything you tell me. What concerns are you experiencing?" This initial prompt taps into the PS's social context and surrounding environment.

TABLE 2.1.   LIBRE Model Ground Rules

Role	Commitment Defined
Confidentiality	All information will remain protected between the problem solver and the facilitator; the only exception if the problem solver poses risk to self or others
Safety	The LIBRE Model problem solving exchange occurs within the problem solver's contextualized safety; the problem solver must feel safe to problem solve so the definition and safety requirements are established before beginning the session
Independence	The goal of the LIBRE Model is to develop problem solving independence; the problem solving is facilitated and modeled with the expectation the problem solver will soon direct and manage all LIBRE Model sessions
Openness	The problem solver is encouraged to speak freely within the problem solving session. The facilitator listens and records responses to the problem solving without offer thoughts or opinions to any content presented within the problem solving exchange.

Problem Solving Self-Efficacy is the ultimate goal; this involves the management of established problem solving skill. The facilitator teaches and models the implement problem solving

Theoretical Underpinning. Bandura (2001, 2006) explains that persons are active agents in their own lives. There are no passive persons to the daily interactions that occur within one's own being. This introductory prompt encourages the first of many self-reflections and the additional incentive is to address any topics that may be unique to the individual. The facilitator's role, as scribe, is designed to record the PS's attentiveness and model the implementation of the LIBRE Model exchange. The facilitators introduce each cue without interjecting their own thoughts or words to the PS's exchange. Deci et al. (1991) explain that there are control distinctions in self-determination. The LIBRE Model prompts are designed to provide the participant the series of self-determined "calls to attention," specifically directing the individual to attend to "self." The responses are recorded as "hair" on the LMSF; see LIBRE Model Stick Figure 2.1.

The facilitator, who is trained to actively listen without judgment or interruption, offers the prompt and waits for Jan to speak. Jan begins, "There is a lot going on right now; My mom works two jobs so that I can go to school; I work one job too; college is expensive, and my manager wants me to pick-up an additional shift. I feel selfish by not working more but with finals coming up, I don't know how I can do more. I'm tired all the time. That's it."

The facilitator restates what she has just recorded and asks if Jan wants to add anything else. Jan shakes her head and says, "No, that's about it for now."

I—Identify a focal Concern. The LIBRE Model exchange continues. The problem-solving pace reflects that of the PS; as she responds quickly to each of the five steps, the facilitator follows that same pace. Jan identifies a concern that she would be willing to process. The facilitator states the second prompt, the identification of a concern and continues: "Of everything that you have identified as concerns, which one would you like for us to address during this time together? Let's write that concern as a question. What would that question be?" The facilitator invites the respondent to review the recorded concerns and focus on one item. The PS gives no additional instruction with the anticipation that she will attend to a self-identified goal. Schunk (1990) explains the importance of setting a goal in self-regulated learning and self-efficacy (Hsieh et al., 2012). The LIBRE Model identified challenge operates as the identified goal for the problem-solving exchange. This question, when specific, becomes the goal that facilitates self-investment. Jan is quick to state, "How can I finish my semester strong?" This response is added to the LMSF shoulders. Once the focal question is identified, the facilitator continues.

B—Brainstorming. The brainstorming prompt follows: "In response to the question you identified, list all possible solutions that you can think of and make sure that you consider realistic and nonrealistic solutions." Brainstorming is a creative task; divergent thinking guides the PS to imagine without restriction (Isaksen & Gaulin, 2005). The responses are recorded on the left side of the LMSF.

Jan begins, "I could stop working; stop sleeping; hire a tutor; quit school; give-up; create a schedule; get organized." Once the respondent generates ideas, the

16 • TEACHER CANDIDATE PROBLEM-SOLVING ENGAGEMENT STYLES

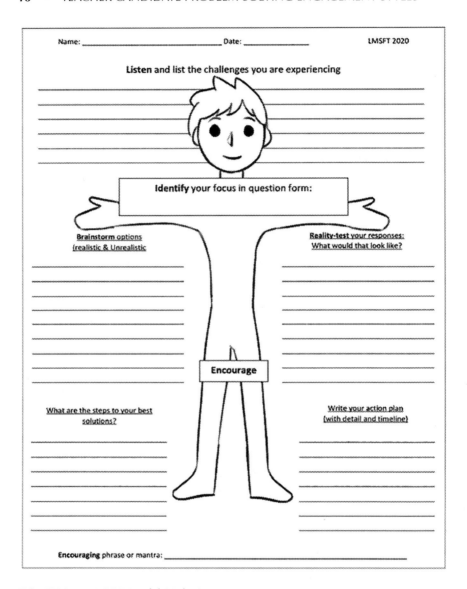

FIGURE 2.1. LIBRE Model Stick Figure

facilitator continues, "Let's now eliminate all non-preferred options and prioritize the ones that remain." Jan decides to keep only two of her generated options. She prioritizes her first as "create a schedule" and her second option as "get organized.

R—Reality-testing. Transitioning to the reality testing and the right-hand side of the LMSF, the facilitator offers the reality-testing prompt, "Let's now further examine the two remaining options. If you were to go forward with the remaining options, what would that look like?" This prompt introduces a time to abstractly imagine behavioral steps and the implications should the respondent pursue the remaining options as actions. Johnson-Laird (1999) explains the abstract reasoning skill as an exploration and clarification of thought, perceptions, and assertions.

Jan continues, "I would need to buy a calendar" and "write everything down to see where my time is going and then make changes if I need to change." She pauses, then continues, "I could organize from there." Once the PS has had time to explain the impact of each option, the next step is the action plan, Encourage step. The facilitator reviews the recorded steps with Jan and then explains the final step.

E—Encourage. The Encourage prompt has two associated components, the first prompt is: (1) "Listing the steps to your best solution." These responses are recorded on the left foot of the stick figure and the second (2) "What are timelines for the completion of each step?" Responses are recorded. Action plan items are recorded with projected completion dates.

Jan quickly states, "(1) buy a calendar; (2) organize my work and school schedule; (3) plan my next day the night before so all I have to do is to follow my schedule." Her timeline, "(1) today after work; (2) tonight when I get home from work; I could even share it with my mom so that she will see how limited my time is and she will know that I am doing my best; (3) then every night before I go to bed, I will review by schedule, what I did and what I will do the next day to make sure I use my time well." The facilitator restates her plan and explains that this completes the LIBRE Model problem-solving.

Theoretical Underpinning. Goal theory explains the importance of developing a plan toward goal acquisition. Goals must be identified, examined and plans developed to orient the person toward goal accomplishment. Self-efficacy and self-regulation are also observable in the outlined process of problem identification and in the development of a resolution plan. How Jan sees herself in addressing the problem reflects her self-efficacy; her steps address her actions. How she regulates and orders those steps provide information about her self-regulation. The LIBRE Model closes as the facilitator asks her to self-reflect and offers her a word of encouragement or a mantra. This final exchange closes the problem-solving session. This is also an invitation to self-reflect and affirms the problem-solving investment that has occurred. The facilitator asks, "what word would you offer yourself as encouragement for the completion of this plan?" This final response acknowledges the PS' attentiveness to the identified problem and the development of a self-regulated action plan (Guerra, 2015). Jan smiles and says, "I can do this!" This final expression is then added below the feet of the LMSF as they close the session.

The participant's task focus is observable in the responses to each prompt. Dweck (2006) explains openness to change is reflective of a growth mindset, which reflects efforts to explore and learn, and that can be observed in the language used. Jan's problem-solving reflects this type of growth mindset; she was willing to see her problem, explore her options and develop a plan to change. Jan's attentiveness to "self" provided her a moment for self-reflection. She was willing to see opportunity and pursue change not as threats, rather as a positive growth option. Had Jan not had a growth mindset, she may not have been willing to even explore the possibility of making a change to her daily life course.

Pintrich (2004) explains that goal achievement behaviors and learning stem from one's beliefs and cognitive processes. Attention helps in improving skills (Ames, 1987). In reflecting on Jan's problem-solving exchange, we again note Jan's willingness to explore her problem, to identify a problem. This problem reflected her beliefs and cognitive investment as she attended to the problem and herself. Jan's solution came as she slowed down her assessment to consider divergent thinking in brainstorming and convergent thinking in reality-testing.

Problem-Solving Is the Sum of Its Parts. As this distinct theoretical model emerges, we can examine the social, cognitive and behavioral investment, goal orientation, and personal agency to the problem-solving activity. Bandura's social cognitive theory is identifiable. The triarchic reciprocity expressed with the PS's listening to self provides insight into her environment, a snapshot into her worldview. As Jan brainstorms, she discloses her personal beliefs, values, and personal expressions of *self*. We see her as a person with her values, beliefs, and culture. Within reality-testing, we see Jan's behavioral investment. Her efficacy in problem-solving provides a unique picture of herself, and her personal agency is visible in her defined challenge (Bandura, 2006).

Goal orientation theory explains the importance of identifying a problem. Goal acquisition cannot occur without a specific goal; similarly, a goal cannot be achieved without a plan and timeline. As Bronfenbrenner (1986) explains, an individual is a combination of the nested experiences that occur over a lifetime of exchanges. The LIBRE Model problem-solving exchange notes these problems.

Concluding Considerations. Problem-solving is an expression of attentiveness. The question to consider is: If we offer the same problem-solving prompts, then why are there diverse response patterns to the individual's identified role, context, and challenge? The response is that the person attends to what he or she wants to address; the challenge, role, and context are for the PS to define. We record initial attention to social cognitive expressions and sustained attention as goal-expressions, that should be managed so that the automaticity reflected within problem-solving can be better understood.

The focus of the LIBRE Model exchange is to address the identified challenge and context of the challenge as stated by the PS; to examine the attention expressed in response to each prompt and to track the developed resolution plan. Initial attention (the Listen/list—Identify—Brainstorm—Reality-testing responses) and the sustained attention (Encourage responses) combine to highlight patterns—engagement styles.

Problem-solving provides important information. What is attended to, how it is attended to, and the willingness to consider change options is only the beginning of the data that one can draw. The LIBRE Model highlights individual intricacies as strength-based reflections. There are inherent vulnerabilities involved in problem-solving that must be considered. For the individual that does not select to change or consider change, there is yet another story. While the same problem-solving prompts are offered to all participants, not all participants respond with the willingness to consider change/resolution.

REFERENCES

Ames. (1987). The enhancement of student motivation. In M. L. Maehr & D. A. Kleiber (Eds.), *Advances in motivation and achievement* (Vol. 5, pp. 123–148). JAI Press.

Bandura, A. (2001). Social cognitive theory: An agentic perspective. *Annual Review of Psychology, 52*, 1–26.

Bandura, A. (2006). Toward a psychology of human agency. *Perspectives on Psychological Science, 1*(2), 164–180.

Bronfenbrenner, U. (1986). Ecology of the family as a context for human development: *Research perspectives, Developmental psychology, 22*(6), 723–742.

Deci, E. L., Vallerand, R. J., Pelletier, L. G., & Ryan, R. M. (1991). Motivation and education: The self-determination perspective. *Educational Psychologist, 26*(3–4), 325–346.

Duda, R., & Shortliffe, E. H. (1983). Expert systems research. *Science, 220*, 261–268.

Dweck, C. (2006). *Mindset: The new psychology of success*. Random House.

Guerra, N. S. (2001). *LIBRE Model.* Unpublished manuscript.

Guerra, N. S. (2009). LIBRE stick figure tool: Graphic organizer. *Interventions in Schools and Clinics, 44*(4), 1–5.

Guerra, N. S. (2015). *Clinical problem-solving case management*. Rowman & Littlefield and Lexington Books.

Hsieh, P., Sullivan, J. R., & Guerra, N. S. (2012). Undergraduate engineering students, beliefs, coping strategies, and academic performance: *An evaluation of theoretical models. Journal of Experimental Education, 80*(2), 196–218.

Isaksen, S. G., & Gaulin, J. P. (2005). A reexamination of brainstorming research: Implications for research and practice. *Gifted Child Quarterly, 49*, 315–329.

Johnson-Laird, P. N. (1999). Deductive reasoning. *Annual Review of Psychology, 50*, 109–135.

Kaufman, S. B. (2020). *Transcend: The new science of self-actualization*. TracherPerigee.

Larkin, J., McDermott, J., Simon, D. P., & Simon, H. A. (1980). Expert and novice performance in solving physics problems. *Science, 208*, 125–134.

Pintrich, P. (2004). A conceptual framework for assessing motivation and self-regulated learning in college students. *Educational Psychology Review, 16*, 385–407.

Schunk, D. (1990). Goal setting and self-efficacy during self-regulated learning. *Educational Psychologist, 25*, 71–86.

CHAPTER 3

ENGAGEMENT STYLE IS THE COMBINATION OF INITIAL AND SUSTAINED ATTENTION

This chapter continues the discussion of the LIBRE Model to explain how embedded theory found within the problem-solving exchange can be used to introduce the concept of engagement styles (Guerra, 2009). The LIBRE Model is host to social cognitive and goal-orientation theories. Individuals' initial attention (IA) is visible as they enter the problem-solving dialogue and sustained attention (SA) can be seen as they continue with the exchange, visible with their noted resolution and investment detail. The resultant engagement style artifact is the combination of the problem-solver's IA and SA responses to context. A discussion of context sets the stage for the presentation of engagement styles.

Maslow refers to deficiency, D-needs (D-realm) mechanisms to protect self; versus grow needs, growth-wisdom, Being-Realm of existence (B-realm) where choices lead to greater integration and wholeness (Kaufman, 2020). As engagement styles are considered, motivation and investment are also variables that influence; what one attends to and how one attends is reflected in selected engagement styles. If as Maslow suggests, the D-needs impact development to hinder growth, and for the B-realm to facilitate growth, context is a likely factor.

Teacher Candidate Problem-Solving Engagement Styles:
LIBRE Model Self-Management Analysis, pages 21–30.
Copyright © 2022 by Information Age Publishing
www.infoagepub.com
All rights of reproduction in any form reserved.

21

Context. The human experience is socially oriented; we begin life in community and grow from that beginning. Almost without exception, we are born and raised with others around us. Bandura (2006) explains that there are no "observers to life"; each is an active participant, agent. Even a more passive participant is selecting to live in that reflexive fashion. Social exchanges assist with the human development and self-identity experiences. Examples of early development include the foundational ground rules established in the home, with family and/or caregivers, who influence communication and behavior. Culture, values, beliefs, and the ascribed attentiveness to each are learned in those early experiences and these contexts have significant impact. Bronfenbrenner (1986) explains that when we examine the individual, we are examining a microsystem or individual-within-a-unit. He describes this as nested dolls to suggest that persons cannot be seen without the context from which the individual resides.

For example, the child born and living in a violent family system. She is taught very early to be quiet and stay out of the way. By the time she is eight when she arrives home from school, she quickly starts dinner and cares for her younger brother and sister. She is hyper-vigilant in caring for them; however, weekends are difficult. Her parents use alcohol and drugs on the weekend; they often become violent. She knows that if she and her siblings hide, they will be safe. Over time, she became attentive to this weekend routine. A new church community initiative has given her and her siblings a new experience; they now all go to the church after-school center until 6:00 p.m. when the bus comes to take them home. She enjoys this daily predictable lifestyle. At the church, she plays, does her homework, and she does not have to worry about her younger brother and sister. That is, until the weekend; then the haunting, associated drinking, and potential violence returns. Her solution is to cry. As such Monday through Thursday, she is happy to jump onto the bus; she is ready to go home. Once Friday arrives, she cries at having to leave the daycare.

One of the daycare workers decides to investigate this unusual behavior; she speaks to the younger brother and sister. In a matter of factual manner tone, they quickly explain, "She cries every weekend. My Dad tells my Mom to take us to our Grandma's or a neighbor, so they do not have to hear her. So, then mom take us to someone's house, and we don't come back home until the weekend is over." To an outsider, this may look, psychologically odd, it may look like an unstable environment. However, what has occurred are a series of learned attentiveness behaviors that have facilitated safety for this young girl and her siblings. Context is critical.

LIBRE MODEL

The *initial* and *sustained attention* are tracked across the continuum of multiple sub-skills found in problem-solving. The associated theory is found in sub-set skills (e.g., self-reflection, abstract thinking, goal setting) and combined to provide a snapshot of the individual's self-managed attention, and problem-solving engagement style.

Initial attention. The LIBRE Model opening prompts feature the respondent's social cognitive experience. The individual speaks to personal-worldview issues and impact. Brainstorming allows a focus on the individual's perceptions: what is possible, what is impossible, probable, and what could be considered in problem-solving. The individual offers information of "self." The person uses this space to address culture, values, and efficacy. Once completed, the reality-testing space focuses on probable behaviors associated with each prioritized option. The individual is given time to reflect before moving forward to develop a resolution.

Bandura's (1986, 2006) active agent descriptive is of a triadic reciprocal social cognitive interaction, which is foundational to the LIBRE Model. The individual is in a constant state of internal and external dialog with self and between the environment, behavior, and the person as perceived in anyone setting. Each person is a "self and culture" as a part of "who" and "how" one operates. Therefore, as conflict arises from social and community interaction so also does the problem-solving opportunity. These established socialized expressions are found as the problem-solver expresses that *initial attention* (See Figure 3.1 Initial Attention Theoretical Framework).

Bandura's (1986) social cognitive reciprocity provides understanding to the differing moments in time and how life is experienced within the eyes of the individual. The recognized value placed upon the problem-solver's environment, personal values, and behavioral views facilitate in the understanding of the opening responses to the "Listen," "Brainstorm," and "Reality-test" responses. The person's perspective, however, extends beyond the problem environment. Once the initial problem (within the embedded context) is presented, the examination of the problem becomes the focus. The presented problem and investment are observable in the detail to the problem presentation. For example, does the person state the problem as "within" or "outside" their control? "How am I going to study for the test?" versus "How am I going to get my boyfriend to help me study for the test?"

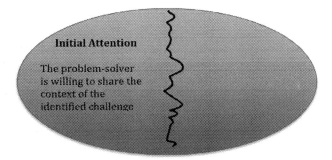

FIGURE 3.1. Initial Attention Theoretical Framework

24 • TEACHER CANDIDATE PROBLEM-SOLVING ENGAGEMENT STYLES

This problem presentation reflects goal orientation which is expressed in how the goal(s) are managed. Sustained attention is noted with the continued goal investment. The problem solver's language and detail in developing the problem resolution plans reflects personal investment. Goal acquisition, similarly, is found in accountability. The problem-solver who is willing to set-up resolution steps and timelines is more likely willing to follow-through and complete those stated plans.

Sustained Attention. Goal-orientation theory assists with understanding motivational investment toward change. Pintrich (2000) explains the importance of goals in originating the person's beliefs and cognitive processing of action toward effects. Bandura (1982) refers to this as self-efficacy, the self-belief in ability to organize and implement action within a specific area. Goal orientation theory values the motivational investment to act moving forward to complete the identified task. Zimmerman (2000) reports the importance of a clearly defined goal in supporting change. Schunk and Ertmer (2000) explain that goal orientation is a management feature to goal acquisition. Clearly defined goals are associated with self-regulated behavior and increased gain.

The LIBRE Model, *I—identification of a problem* provides similar goal development features. The more clearly defined the problem is stated, the more likely the motivational attention is that the problem-solver will sustain investment to develop a resolution plan. For example, if the student identifies her problem as being hungry, this specific information suggests an investment in this problem. As she continues, she says that she is going to get a hamburger before she arrives home so that she does not have to make dinner. This specificity supports her identified challenge/goal.

The *I—identification of a problem* challenge is written as a question to provide the respondent the space to develop the goal with next steps. To restate, the more succinct the goal, the greater the likelihood for sustained attention, motivation toward the goal and greater probability that the resolution will be developed to meet that goal (See Figure 3.2 Sustained Attention Theoretical Framework).

Let's look at examples of this applied theory application within the LIBRE Problem-Solving Model exchanges.

Actual Engagement Style. Alice is open and welcomes the opportunity to visit with the LIBRE Model facilitator. They visit briefly before the facilitator addresses the goal of the meeting: to problem solve. Alice smiles and the facilitator continues with the presentation of ground rules. Alice asks questions such as, "I can problem solve any challenge? It doesn't have to be about school? Do I get to keep a copy of whatever we discuss?" Once all of her questions have been answered, the facilitator offers the first prompt, L—listen and list. By this time Alice is ready; she speaks as the facilitator records her responses. "I am a non-traditional student; I began at the community college before transferring to the University." She continues, "I have been married for three years, I have one child, I love school." "But money is tight." "We want to be good parents." "My husband

Engagement Style is the Combination of Initial and Sustained Attention • 25

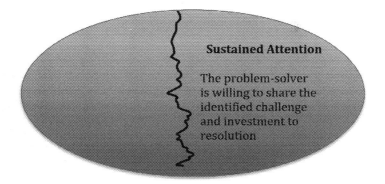

FIGURE 3.2. Sustained Attention Theoretical Framework

works two jobs and I work one job just to make ends meet." "We want the best for our daughter and for our family."

Once all of her responses have been recorded, they move to the next prompt, I—identify a concern. "Of everything you have identified as concerns, which one would you like for us to explore during this time together?" Alice's response is immediate, "time." The facilitator asks that she create a question, and Alice states, "How do I balance my time?"

The third prompt, B—brainstorm, moves quickly when Alice lists: "don't worry, worry, quit school, quit work, organize." She hesitates and then reports, "Plan." Together, they eliminate those options that were only part of the brainstorming activity; they prioritize the remaining options before continuing.

The fourth prompt is R—reality testing. The facilitator invites Alice to imagine going forward with each of the remaining options. "What would it look like if you actually did go forward with each?" Alice only had two options remaining after eliminating and prioritizing her possible solutions. She begins, "Plan—I am going to have to sit down and look at everything that is going on at work, at home, with my husband, with my baby. Organize—once I have maybe listed everything (like we are doing now), then I need to organize and set up a new plan."

The final prompt is intended to encourage and allow the respondent a space to develop their resolution. The facilitator states, "Let's list the steps to your best solution." "Great! I need to: (1) buy a calendar, (2) set-up a time to talk to my husband, (3) list everything that we both involved in at work and at home, (4) plan our work and school time, (5) plan our time together and with Kali." The facilitator continues, "This is a great list; now let's add timelines for accountability. Tell me when you are going to: (1) buy a calendar?" Alice is quick to see where they are going, so she responds to each listed step: (1) today after work, (2) after dinner tonight when we are both home from work, (3) next week, Friday, so we can both think about everything and prepare, (4) the following Friday and (5) that

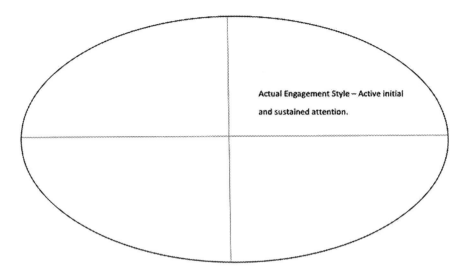

FIGURE 3.3. Actual Engagement Style

same Friday." Alice is pleased with herself so when the facilitator asks her to offer herself a positive word or mantra, she quickly says, "I can do this!"

The actual engagement style is self-reflective, with a heightened sense of self in relation and attuned to the environment. When invited to problem solve, the individual provides a personalized structure to address all that has been whirling around in her head. See Figure 3.3 Actual Engagement Style; this graphic is organized with goal focused engagement and actual engagement styles on the top as higher order active engagement, while the engagement styles displayed on the bottom were intended to show lower activity and limited engagement activity. Goal focused engagement is organized as diagonal from venting engagement as they are perceived as opposites in terms of outcomes, similarly to how actual engagement is viewed as opposite of potential engagement. As one student said, after having filled two sheets of paper with everything that was occurring in his life, "Can I keep these sheets? Everything is now organized and I'm ready to go."

Potential Engagement Style. The opposite engagement style to actual is potential. Polly enters the problem-solving exchange with a timid demeanor. The facilitator welcomes her and after a brief conversation explains the opportunity to problem solve and the associated ground rules. Polly smiles. The facilitator offers the first prompt and Polly is silent. After a long pause, Polly says, "I don't have any problems and when I do, I just tell my Mom and she tells me what to do." The facilitator visits with her again and after reflecting on her shared worldview, the facilitator thanks her for visiting with her. The session closes with the facilitator asking Polly to offer herself a positive word. She smiles and says, "Thank you."

Engagement Style is the Combination of Initial and Sustained Attention • 27

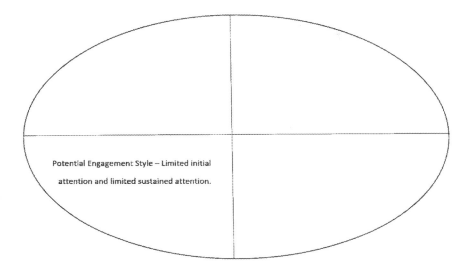

FIGURE 3.4. Potential Engagement Style

The potential engagement style is suggestive of someone who is not willing to engage or selects not to engage. Of course, other possibilities should be considered, however the end product is the same. This person is filtering shared information (See 3.4 Potential Engagement Style). These persons may be tied to cultural values that will not allow them to speak of problems outside the home or they may not know how to problem solve. Considerations that will need to be addressed as engagement styles are explored.

Goal-focused Engagement Style. Greg enters the problem-solving exchange with little interest in addressing his immediate daily environment. After ground rules are explained, he explains to the facilitator that he already knows what he wants to talk about, so he wants to begin. She agrees; they move from the initial prompt to the second, I—identify the concern. The facilitator asks him to create the concern as a question and his reply is immediate, "How do I find a doctor?"

The third prompt is offered, "In response to the question you identified, list all possible solutions, and let's make sure that you think of realistic and nonrealistic solutions." "Okay. I could ask other students in my class; use the telephone book; call insurance; I could drive around; I could Google doctors by zip code; ask my professor." They then eliminated those non-working options and prioritized the remaining. Greg's reality testing considers: (1) call insurance—ask the insurance to send a list of doctors; (2) the drive around option was extended to consider driving around in his area so that he does not select a doctor that is across town. And his final option is (3) to Google doctors that were in his zip code and see if they were on the insurance listing.

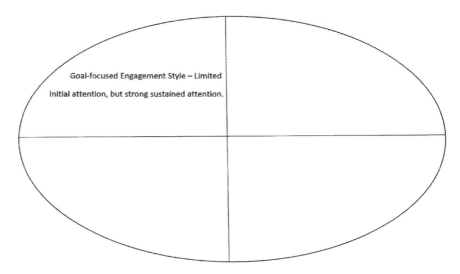

FIGURE 3.5. Goal-focused Engagement Style

They then moved to the E—encourage prompt of listing the best solution and timelines for accomplishing each. Greg's plan and timeline are as follows:

(1) Contact the insurance company and ask them to send the listing of doctors by email
(1) Today after class

(2) Identify two doctors that are in the area and on the list
(2) Tomorrow

(3) Call and set-up interview appointments
(3) Select the first opening appointments

(4) Write up questions and interview doctors
(4) Over the next two weeks

(5) Make a decision and select a doctor
(5) By February 1st

Greg offered himself a word of encouragement—a mantra. His response was without hesitation: "I've got this."

The goal-focused engagement style is solution focused. While there is little interest in speaking of addressing the larger context, the personal investment is to the identified need and how best to address it (See 3.5 Goal-focused Engagement Style).

Engagement Style is the Combination of Initial and Sustained Attention • 29

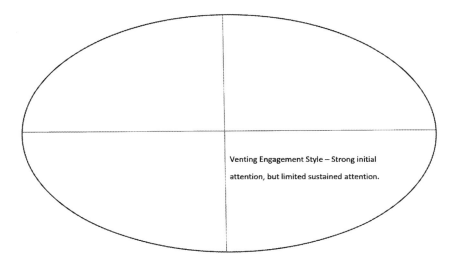

FIGURE 3.6. Venting Engagement Style

Venting Engagement Style. The final engagement style is that of venting. Stylistically, it begins in similar fashion to an actual engagement style. The individual is actively involved in sharing the personal-worldview, context, and the problem, but this is where things change. The venting engagement style individual wants to share the problem but has no interest in resolution. Often the identified problem is outside his/her control. So even if there was an initial investment because they have positioned themselves outside "self" they are able to identify that it is beyond their control to be responsible. Vince is invited to problem solve and he is excited to begin the process. Once the ground rules are shared, he begins listing his concerns: "My mom is mad at my grandma; school is so demanding; I have homework every night; no time to visit friends or family; I feel like I don't have a social life anymore."

The second prompt was offered to Vince. He smiled and said, "How do I get my mom and grandma to stop fighting?" With this question presented, he continues. His brainstorming includes: "I could tell my mom not to fight with grandma; I could tell grandma to not fight with mom; I could do nothing; I could tell them to stop talking to each other." Vince indicated that he would eliminate doing nothing. His prioritizing was "(1) tell my mom not to fight with grandma, (2) tell grandma to not fight with mom, (3) tell them to stop talking to each other." As Vince began to reality test, he continued with repeating what he had already offered. "I just need to tell mom not to talk with grandma and tell grandma not to talk to mom." His E—encourage prompt was a continuation. "I just need to tell them to stop talking to each other." His timeline, "I don't really know when I am going to have the time to visit with each of them because I am so busy with school." Vince was asked to offer himself a word of encouragement/mantra. He offered, "I am

30 • TEACHER CANDIDATE PROBLEM-SOLVING ENGAGEMENT STYLES

not going to worry about it." The venting engagement style is more invested in the narrative of the problem and less on the resolution, (See Figure 3.6 Venting Engagement Style).

Concluding Engagement Style Thoughts. The LIBRE Model provides a view of engagement (actual) and non-engagement (potential) along with the two gradient versions of engagement (venting—initially invested and goal-focused—solution invested). These distinct attentiveness patterns are visible in the language and specificity used to problem solve. Their investment is seen in their resolutions and the detail offered with their plans and timelines, which support their personal accountability.

Maslow's Needs vs. Growth. Maslow's hierarchy of needs has a point to offer. For Polly, the potential, and Vince, the venting engagement style, each has selected or assumed a deficient need approach. Polly does not attend or participate in her social setting; a context that does not provide safety or security; similarly, Vince, while he initially seems invested, presents a problem that is not only not his problem but a problem that he has absolutely no control to manage. Thus, their need as presented is sustained as a deficient need that cannot be addressed.

Alice, on the other hand, is actual in her engagement style. She is conscious, aware, and reflective of her changing environment and context. Her wisdom leads her to take steps to set her up for further participation and success. Greg with his goal-focused engagement is compelled to focus on next actions. Growth and change in the wisdom he crafted lead and motivated him.

REFERENCES

Bandura, A. (1982). Self-efficacy mechanism in human agency. *American Psychologist, 37*, 122–147.

Bandura, A. (1986). *Social foundations of thought and action: A social cognitive theory.* Pearson Education Company Prentice-Hall.

Bandura, A. (2006). Toward a psychology of human agency. *Perspectives on Psychological Science, 1*(2), 164–180.

Bronfenbrenner, U. (1986). Ecology of the family as a context for human development: Research Perspective. *Developmental Psychology, 22*(6), 723–742.

Guerra, N. S. (2009). LIBRE stick figure tool: Graphic organizer. *Interventions in School and Clinic, 44*(4), 1–5.

Guerra, N. S. (2009). Illustrations of engagement styles: Four teacher candidates. *Teacher Education and Practice, 22*(1), 43–57.

Kaufman, S. B. (2020). *Transcend: The new science of self-actualization.* TracherPerigee.

Pintrich, P. R. (2000). Multiple goals, multiple pathways: The role of goal orientation in learning and achievement. *Journal of Educational Psychology, 92*, 544–555.

Schunk, D. H., & Ertmer, P. A. (2000). Self-regulation and academy learning. Self-efficacy enhancing intervention. In M. Boekaerts, P. R. Pintrich, & M. Zeidner (Eds.), *Handbook of self-regulation* (pp. 631–649). American Press.

Zimmerman, B. (2000). The development of scientific skills. *Development Review, 20*, 99–149.

CHAPTER 4

AN ECOLOGICAL LOOK AT IDENTITY AND RESILIENCE INTERSECTIONALITY

APA Multicultural Model

Daily living involves social-cognitive contexts, culture, and assumed roles mediated by community. Individual identities transition as the person moves from one place to another. We can see how people manage their identity by the ways in which they allocate their time and attention, particularly in response to pressing demands. Self-management is visible in these attention allocations and responses. For example, a teacher candidate reports that his everyday life is stressful. He is experiencing continued duress. Observed, we see his heightened attention and clarity to his perceived stressful conditions and identified challenge. The teacher explains that he has created a problem-solving strategy to address his challenging experiences. When asked to explain, he immediately details the development of his resolution plan. He begins by defining his stressful role within his individualized social context, this awareness helps him manage and engage in the problem resolution. He adjusts his attention (from venting and feeling helpless) to an ac-

Teacher Candidate Problem-Solving Engagement Styles:
LIBRE Model Self-Management Analysis, pages 31–37.
Copyright © 2022 by Information Age Publishing
www.infoagepub.com
All rights of reproduction in any form reserved.

32 • TEACHER CANDIDATE PROBLEM-SOLVING ENGAGEMENT STYLES

tual engagement style that addresses his role and context and provides him control of the management of his context.

This chapter explores the following language to address these crossroads: (1) self-reported identity and identity intersectionality, (2) contexts and conflict, (3) engagement, and (4) observed resilience. To begin, we will discuss the APA 2017 Multicultural Guidelines (2017) and follow up with a created segue to consider relational resilience as a sustained support for health transition and whole person development.

APA Multicultural Guidelines of an Ecological Approach to Context, Identity, and Intersectionality. Sue and colleagues' (1982) research on cross-cultural counseling was the basis for the original 2002 American Psychological Association (APA) Model. Bronfenbrenner's (1977, 1979) human development ecological model of nested expanding layered systems was introduced to the re-worked framework in 2017; this human experience inclusion was notable to the expanded multicultural guidelines. The 2017 multicultural definition was also extended to include: age, generation, culture, language, gender, race, ethnicity, ability status, sexual orientation, gender identity, socioeconomic status, religion, spirituality, immigration status, education and employment identities (Clauss-Ehlers et al., 2013). New counseling research (Ratts et al., 2016), social work (National Association of Social Workers, 2015), and others' cultural competency research findings were added.

While the original APA model provides a guide for psychologists working with diverse clients, these guidelines are pertinent and applicable to all educators who are preparing teachers to work with diverse populations. This chapter adapts the guidelines to address the educational setting with the subtle introduction of the ethical professional standard, to cause no harm.

Guideline 1. Importance of identity and self-definition as fluid and complex. The human development experience is fluid. Individuals mature along a continuum, however at different rates as intersections arise among their multiple roles. To illustrate, let's consider a young woman growing-up in a traditional Latino intact family. Her family memberships include her mother, father, and four siblings. After completing school in her home community and school district, she decides to go to college in another city. This decision introduces significant changes to her cultural ecological system. Her home cultural experiences are different from the new academic setting. Her home language is Spanish, and her social family context and community are different from her new expected performance in this higher education setting. English is the only language spoken in this new setting and the individuality of competition in the classroom and outside the classroom are its primary values. Her identity has changed.

There is a complexity as the young woman finds that her survival is dependent upon her developing a new identity that embraces these new values to thrive. The year passes quickly, and she is successful. However, there are consequences to this fluid intersectionality, including the new identity that quickly challenges her

An Ecological Look at Identity and Resilience Intersectionality • **33**

as she returns home. Now she must again adjust herself from her emerging college student identity or risk rejection from her home cultural identity as daughter and sibling. Awareness of multiple identities is painful. She initially felt isolated following her move from home until she learned how to fit into the college higher education system. Now that she is returning home, her school identity and values are incongruent, and she struggles to reconnect with family and friends. Her self-identification is fluid and complex.

Guideline 2. Cultural attitudes and beliefs influence perception. Individuals grow-up within a context that includes language, values, mores/customs, and tenets that shape and influence their worldviews. Bias and distinct views likewise influence their acquired knowledge and experiences. We return to the young Latina; she developed language, culture, and values that are distinct to her home community. As she steps into a new world of higher education and its many experiences, she begins integrating these perceptions into the new setting. Her views influence her cultural attitudes and beliefs. She must adjust her views to accommodate and shift away from her early perceptions to develop new perspectives. Her perceptions are influenced by cultural attitudes and beliefs.

Guideline 3. Engagement is in language and communication. Language is significant to communication and engagement. Our young Latina, who learned English as a second language, holds a fundamental value to Spanish as the first language she learned and to her cultural heritage. Her primary Spanish language, and home values make-up her secure foundation. Similarly, her engagement to her language and culture provided a strong self-efficacy. Her earliest communications were in Spanish. Communication and the values she learned were in Spanish. As she moves away from home, language and culture, she faces a shift toward a new identity with a different language and associated values. Language influences engagement, which is significant to communication. What she attends to and how she directs her attention are challenged as she attempts to create the secure balance that she held at home.

Guideline 4. Social and physical context influence views of environment. Social exchange and accompanying physical context set the stage for what the individual sees, and the interpretations assumed. Our young Latina is timid within the higher educational experience; this new context hampers her initial engagement and perception. Her social interactions with peers appear awkward as she struggles to learn the expectations of this new social context within this foreign physical setting. From an outside observer, she does not appear engaged; for her, the goal is to appear as someone who does "fit" into the successful college student community. This could lead to an internal and external "at-risk" designation; internal as she struggles with herself and external as she observes her advisor within the context of her role as a student. The complexities of her new environment are influencing her identity development.

Guideline 5. Historical and contemporary experiences with power, privilege, and oppression. Similarly, for the Latino family who came to the United States only to find further oppression, this creates subtle views that leave the family again feeling victimized and not empowered. Family values extend onto the individual family members. The individual members gain a perspective as a collective that they should not trust those who are different from themselves. Our Latina student, meanwhile, seeks social exchanges to learn about her new higher education environment. She wants to engage in this new setting but does not know how. Therefore, she is inclined to stay to herself; thereby slowing down her learning curve in addressing both historical and contemporary experiences of power, privilege, and oppression. It is here that the teacher holds a major role. What and how teachers assess and invite students to engage is in the hands of teachers who either facilitate or compromise the learning experience.

Guideline 6. Culturally adaptive interventions and advocacy. The importance of this guideline is for individual(s)/educator(s) wanting to assist their students with those associated cultural considerations that affect their educational learning experience. Informed interventions must be considered in meeting the sociocultural needs and partnerships with diverse sociocultural communities. For example, student higher education support systems should consider not only academic support but also engagement support, intervening as challenges occur; offering early intervention toward recovery will assist with students' positive progress. For example, educators should include the importance of context in teaching classroom management and the presentation of new learning.

Teacher candidates need to begin their classroom management with open-ended questions to explore what the students hold as context in complimenting new information. This initial active listening provides a demonstrated respect for the students, their culture, background, and identity; such that, as new experiences are introduced, they are presented in a mutually valued framework.

Guideline 7. Profession's self-examination of assumptions and practices within a global context and the impact upon self-definition, purpose, role, and function. It is important for educators to examine their own cultural bias (positive and negative) and presenting assumptions. Examination of professional practice bias is a prerequisite to modeling cultural inclusiveness. The responsibility of self-reflection is the responsibility of the individual and biases left unexamined can compromise professional roles. For example, the White professor who has an unexamined bias that led her to assess Latino students as lazy and not engaged; these judgements may occur without the professor being aware. Culture and cultural biases are real. Our young Latina, as she is experiencing isolation and loneliness as a first generation and first time away from home student, may appear unengaged when the reality is that she is attempting to understand her new context.

Guideline 8. Developmental stages and life transitions intersect with larger biosociocultural context to influence worldviews and identity. We experience multiple identities; developing and sustaining the awareness of these identities and the changes associated with these experiences, facilitate a person's direction and self-management. Some individuals' lives are lived in these vulnerable spaces. We return to our Latina student who has now graduated. She falls in love and marries someone from a German background. She and her German husband have children that have grown-up in yet a different sociocultural context community. They have moved away from both her and his families. It is not until she returns home for an extended visit that she realizes these new challenges. As she interacts with her family, she recognizes her multiple identities and her task of negotiating changes across each context and identity. She is not only a Latina daughter; she is a wife of a German husband; and mother of multicultural children who have grown up in yet a different multicultural community. Her development and transitions intersect, and her self-awareness facilitates these cultural transitions.

Guideline 9. Culturally appropriate and informed research, teaching, supervision, consultation, and evaluation of efficacy. Educators, like psychologists, have a responsibility to be culturally self-efficacious. Professional development should always include culturally appropriate and informed direct (classroom instruction) and indirect (e.g., consultation) services. Should our Latina student approach a faculty member, there is the expectation that the faculty is aware of the student's intersectionality of identity, context, and engagement, and the influencing factors. To assist the student's development of resilience, a teacher-student relationship is essential. Without this support, she may find herself back to victimizing perceptions expressed within her home culture; she should have remained home to her cultural role and identity. Her resiliency is necessary to move from trauma toward positive relational support. She assures herself of her skill to learn and develop the needed supports to be successful and to thrive.

Guideline 10. Educators, like psychologists, should seek strength-based approaches to build resilience within sociocultural contexts. Zimmerman and Brenner (2010) discuss strength-based approaches and the importance of attending to positive context, social, and individual factors that counter the unhealthy aspects to promote healthy development and resilience. Likewise, problem-solving becomes an ideal approach to address, reveal, and support the complex self-reported identity of a person within each of the contexts in which he or she exists, to support positive action-oriented engagement. The goal is for the person to move toward a more positive resolution, thereby supporting the person's resilience.

Resilience provides coping strategies to overcoming challenges. As Clauss-Ehlers (2004) explains, it is the process of working with and working through stress by combining the positive cultural background, values, and sociocultural factors to meet the need from a positive supportive lens. Relational resilience (Jordan, 1992, 2000) extends and emphasizes the interpersonal and contextual roles presented with processing culture and identity. This form of resilience results from mutual engagement, and the successful movement from disconnection to reconnection in relationship (Jordan & Schwartz, 2018).

Relational Resilience. Relational resilience is conceptualized within Relational-Cultural Theory (RCT), which had its earliest beginning with feminist literature. Core RCT concepts include:

a. Personal growth develops through and toward growth-fostering relationships;
b. Movement toward connectedness;
c. Relational differentiation;
d. Mutual empathy and empowerment as core elements to growth-fostered relationships;
e. The value of growth-fostering relationships;
f. Development is for all involved; and
g. As relational development occurs, this also increases competence and capacities (Jordan, 2000).

Increased knowledge and insight, which develop in relation to others, provide perspective to address disconnections from self or others. When people work through disconnections, they can experience and provide support, through mutuality, which helps them be resilient. Therefore, as our young Latina moves across the intersections of identity and within her growth-fostering relationships (Jordan, 1992), her awareness of these movements offer her an additional place to pause. Her relational competency allows her to reflect upon how best to remain connected to those from differing contexts authentically. While they are not directly involved in her current identity, she values them and wishes to maintain the connection to them and to that part of herself. For example, she is now married and living with her new culture and worldview. She still loves her family of birth and acknowledges the cultural values and support they provided. However, she must now be intentionally committed to remain connected to those identity roles that may not have a direct or active relation to her current identity as wife.

SUMMARIZING TO LOOK FORWARD

This chapter presented an Ecological Approach to Context, Identity, and Intersectionality to suggest that educators should frame their teacher candidate instruction with the acknowledged awareness of identity and the demonstrated complexity of context. Now with increased responsibilities placed on teachers to provide the social emotional learning for their students to learn, teacher candidates also need the curricular investment that can be facilitated by relational coaching and problem-solving exchanges.

Professional development is a fluid system of growth and development. As individuals experience changes, so also do their identities; changing contexts can moderate attention and either facilitate or hamper emerging role identities. When people experience stress, they need a context in which to gain resilience. All people involved can benefit when communities and their contexts adapt to their needs. When people experience stress without the resources to manage it, they can experience trauma, particularly if a person has experienced prior trauma.

We will now take these constructs and instruments to examine their application with two masters' teacher candidates. Each has a distinct background and multicultural experience that is reflected in who each is and how each engages in their studies, home, and student teaching experiences.

REFERENCES

American Psychological Association. (2017). *Multicultural guidelines: An ecological approach to context, identity, and intersectionality.* http://www.apa.org/about/policy/multicultural-guidelines.pdf

Bronfenbrenner, U. (1979). *The ecology of human development: Experiments by nature and design.* Harvard University Press.

Bronfenbrenner, U. (1977). Toward an experimental ecology of human development. *American Psychologist, 32*(7), 513–531.

Clauss-Ehlers, C. S. (2004). Re-inventing resilience: A model of culturally-focused resilient adaptation. In C. S. Clauss-Ehlers & M. D. Weist (Eds.), *Community planning to foster resilience in children* (pp. 27–41). Kluwer.

Clauss-Ehlers, C. S., Serpell, Z., & Weist, M. D. (2013). *Handbook of culturally responsive school mental health: Advancing research, training, practice, and policy.* Springer.

Jordan, J. V. (1992). Relational-cultural therapy. *Handbook of counseling women* (pp. 63–73). Springer.

Jordan, J. V. (2000). The role of mutual empathy in relational/cultural therapy. *Journal of Clinical Psychology, 56,* 1005–1016.

Jordan, J., & Schwartz, H. (2018). Radical empathy in teaching. *New Directions for Teaching and Learning, 2018*(153), 25–35. https://doi.org/10.1002/tl.20278

National Association of Social Workers. (2015). *Standards and indicators for cultural competency in social work practice.* Author.

Ratts, M. J., Singh, A. A., Nassar-McMillan, S., Butler, S. K., & McCullough, J. R. (2016). Multicultural and social justice counseling competencies: Guidelines for the counseling profession. *Journal of Multicultural Counseling and Development, 44*(1), 28–48.

Sue, D. W., Bernier, J. E., Durran, A., Feinberg, L., Pedersen, P., Smith, E. J., & Vasquez-Nuttall, E. (1982). Position paper: Cross-cultural counseling competencies. *The Counseling Psychologist, 10,* 45–52.

Zimmerman, M. A., & Brenner, A. B. (2010). Resilience in adolescence: Overcoming neighborhood disadvantage. In J. W. Reich, A. J. Zautra, & J. S. Hall (Eds.), *Handbook of adult resilience* (pp. 283–308). Guilford Press.

SECTION 2

ILLUSTRATIONS OF ENGAGEMENT STYLES

CHAPTER 5

PARTICIPANTS AND RESEARCH PLAN

This chapter outlines the overall presentation of the two case studies. Each participant was a master's graduate student preparing to be a teacher. During the course of their studies, three distinct problem-solving sessions were conducted each year. Three analyses were used to address these participants' data: (1) a review and study of LIBRE Model problem-solving reported challenges, attention/attentiveness, role identification, context, resolution plans and engagement styles; (2) exploration of problem-solvers' intersections of identity/roles, context, engagement and outcomes as processed in using the ecological multicultural model; and (3) an examination of the internal problem-solving dialog (community-of-self) as the two teacher candidates experienced their transformative changes. An action research framework was used to examine the problem-solvers' narratives as separate voices that contribute to a larger understanding of "self-as-group" influenced by culture, context and the interactive exchanges found among a distinct individual with a variety of community roles. While this framework use is uncommon, this structure allows for the articulation of individuals' movement across multiple identities, contexts, and engagement styles in efforts to maintain resiliency. These interpersonal dialog offer much to the understanding of self and the integration of self as a whole person developing professional.

Teacher Candidate Problem-Solving Engagement Styles:
LIBRE Model Self-Management Analysis, pages 41–49.
Copyright © 2022 by Information Age Publishing
www.infoagepub.com
All rights of reproduction in any form reserved.

41

42 • TEACHER CANDIDATE PROBLEM-SOLVING ENGAGEMENT STYLES

These multi-faceted approaches provide an opportunity for systematic study of individuals with the goal of identifying effective solutions to daily-confronted challenges (Stringer, 2004, 2007, 2014). This planned research is structured to describe the complexity and puzzling events that occur in professional preparation and how they simultaneously impact life. For students in transition, preparing to become teachers, the intention is to examine their meaningful and fulfilling work impact as it is communicated through problem solving. The literature reiterates the complexity of the teacher shortage phenomenon; as teacher turnover trends increase, significantly fewer individuals are seeking teacher education degrees (Flores et al., 2018; Holland, 2017). Jacobson et al. (2019) explain education as a complex system. Growing professional concerns and consistent shortages have introduced alternative certification programs. Approaches are offered from a variety of sources, and while all have the same goal to prepare skilled teachers, no one approach has been able to address the complexity of the challenge.

For this study, we used several assumptions to address the teacher candidates' problem solving and psychosocial expressions as they enter and progress through this grant-funded, accelerated masters' teacher preparation program. The intention was to address the teacher candidates as problem-solvers and how the collected data addressed the self, within context, and within multiple self-expressions analogous to a "group self." The anticipation was to better understand the complexity of the teacher candidate experience (as a problem-solver) and with the goal of better understanding the events and management of events that teacher candidates encounter (within self and outside self). The two selected teacher candidates in this study will be systematically interviewed over a two-year period. Their successful culmination was measured with their master's degree completion that included required course work for their certification and employment as a teacher. This problem-solving data tracked their transition from one career to their decision to re-enter school as a graduate student teacher candidate and graduate with certification into their second career as teaching professionals.

CASE STUDY

We selected two cases, each demonstrated a range in attention/engagement style attributes, identity, context, outcomes, and larger pattern of trauma versus resiliency. This narrative presentation will address preferred engagement styles with defined contexts. Noted engagement style differences within each teacher candidate will be examined. A male and female have selected to examine the concept of "attention" within their contextualized roles. We also examined teacher candidate engagement styles, and related resolutions. The first case study is of a female teacher candidate and the second is of a male teacher candidate. Each case study has distinct attention patterns—engagement styles. While not generalizable, each represents common features that affect student roles to introduce the importance of engagement and transitioning advantage of self-awareness on self-management. The researchers were careful to identify individuals from distinct

Participants and Research Plan • **43**

graduate programs; one student was a special education teacher candidate and the other was a math teacher candidate.

ECOLOGICAL STUDY

The ecological evaluation considers the larger context of each teacher candidate as a multicultural person. The APA multicultural ecological model frames this discussion (Claus-Ehlers et al., 2019). The teacher candidates' family systems and cultural differences were considered as they progressed through their programs. The "worldview lens" of each teacher candidate was examined with a focus on their language, role, and attention. The relationships that they expressed with the transitional coach were also examined within the context of relational resiliency. This review was designed to explore how teacher candidates position themselves within their multi-identity and contexts as they move from student to teacher.

ACTION RESEARCH

The action research framework includes: "the identification of a problem or issue to be investigated, a defined process of inquiry and explanations that enable individuals to understand the nature of the problem" (Springer, 2007, p. 4). With this work, we focused on how teacher candidates approached the problem-solving experience. The teacher candidate problem-solving patterns were tracked analogous to a group dynamic. Qualitative research, like action research designs, is not intended to be generalizable. There are, however, some generalizable solution-orientated features and expectations that facilitated adaptability. One example is the role of context. The plan was to examine articulated problems, context, and resolutions through the eyes of the teacher candidates; this data became the *community-of-self* or a self-group expression. This information included information that was presented by the person within the context of their role and identified challenge. The goal was to explore if there were solution-oriented features that facilitated the successful management of their changing profession.

Method. The systematic data research routine included: (1) establishing transitional support for the teacher candidates with a trained (LIBRE Model) counselor; (2) providing a series of problem-solving exchanges to identify challenges encountered. For example, context is critical in action research to provide an understanding of what the person(s) is/are experiencing. The LIBRE Model counselor explains the importance of being present with what is occurring within his/her worldview context.

The LIBRE Model Stick Figure (LMSF) is used to collect data (participant responses), to record the created picture described as the teacher candidate's "worldview" is presented. The established rapport and update begins prior to addressing each new problem/problem-solving exchange. All LIBRE Model problem-solving teacher candidates' sessions were recorded. Only the teacher candidates' words are recorded and placed upon the LMSFs, which functioned as the artifact used to collect data. The scripted L-I-B-R-E cues created a systematic dialog that was repeated with each interview. Data included: revisiting prior identified resolution plans, plan completion and effectiveness, and the introduction of new problem solving (Guerra, 2015).

Attention investment is noted within the presented context and problem identified. The expressed detail and participant investment focused on the problem goal and resolution are used to determine attention investment; (3) recorded problem-solving statements were used to explore and answer the question "what is happening here?" and to interpret and explain the processing; and (4) to act upon the reported plan, implementation, and evaluation (Springer, 2007). The third and fourth steps are a continual process of tracking and reviewing (prior) problem-solving plans with the teacher candidates. Together, the facilitator and teacher candidate reflect on earlier problem-solving experiences to explore the impact of the executed/non-executed plans.

Setting. The data was collected at a designated Hispanic Serving Institution (HSI) University in Texas; one of two public universities located in San Antonio, a southwest metropolitan city. The city also has four private universities and five community colleges along with other technical and online schools. The city demographics include 1.5 million residents of 63.1 percent Hispanic, 26.6 percent White, 7.1 percent Black, 2.4 percent Asian, 0.9 Native American, and 1.2 percent mixed ethnicities. San Antonio is a multicultural city with a large military presence. It has been identified as one of the fastest growing cities; it is the seventh largest city in the United States and is the second largest city in Texas (U. S. Census Bureau, 2010).

Setting Description. The University of Texas at San Antonio (UTSA) student demographic parallels the city. UTSA has five Colleges of which one is the College of Education and Human Development (COEHD). Within the COEHD, there are seven departments, which house 19 graduate programs (4 doctoral and 15 master's programs), and 8 undergraduate programs. There are 4 undergraduate teaching degree programs and 7 graduate teaching degree programs; there is 1 degree at the elementary level and 1 degree at the secondary level (UTSA, 2019).

Participant Selection. Participants were members of this institutional grant focused on preparing teachers to meet high shortage teaching areas. Each of the selected participants received their coursework in a traditional class setting at one of two UTSA campus sites. The main campus is on the northwest side of the city and the second campus is situated in the downtown area of the city, closer to business, city offices and high need low-income schools. This Accelerated Teacher Education Program (ATEP) grant focused on recruiting, preparing, and retaining "highly qualified" graduates, retired military and "*career changers.*" For the purposes of this grant and study, *career changers* were defined as individuals who held an undergraduate degree, however, after completing that initial degree, selected to return to the university to pursue a masters' degree with the teaching certificate.

Each participant had worked in a first career prior to returning to the University to seek a master's degree; however, after having that first career experience, selected to return to school with the intention of becoming a teacher. The primary grant goal was to prepare these candidates to be highly skilled teachers within one year and a half. As an accelerated program, each student would complete the Master of Arts degree and teaching certification requirements within this period of time. "Of the 203 participants, all completed their certification coursework and 56 percent completed a master's degree" (Flores et al., 2018, p. 20). Outside the formal instruction, each student was offered professional development experiences on both the main and downtown campuses. The problem-solving exchanges, which were a component of the transitional coaching, were also received on both campuses.

Baeten and Meeus' (2016) work with career changers was reviewed in the development of the proposed evidence-based services. They suggest that teacher development with career changers requires (1) a preparatory period; (2) allowing space for a transfer of second career teacher expertise into the teaching profession; (3) establishing opportunities for self-directed learning and peer support; (4) integrating coursework with field experience; (5) offering multiple field experiences; (6) extensive mentoring; and (7) allowing for flexibility with the program (p. 180).

Foundation Research Tenet. This consensual inquiry approach built upon a working relationship that fostered the productive communication between the transitional coach (TC) and teacher candidate(s). All the problem-solving exchanges were conducted by the LIBRE Model trained counselor. The counselor and teacher established rapport and ethical ground rules were adhered to at all times. Participants were encouraged to address their personal cultural and psychosocial values; no judgments or comments were given in response to information shared, even as the content of the identified problems were presented. Participants expressed their social identities, represented by class, ethnicity, culture, race, religion, and individual values; they were also able to use the language of their choice in problem-solving. This approach facilitated these communications as the teacher candidates examined change; they noted personal and the larger frame concerns with content (e.g., learning new material) and context (e.g., classroom management). This is research that brings attention to inclusion and ensures that everyone's thoughts are given space to think, speak, and process (Guerra, 2009; Springer, 2007).

The Facilitator as Researcher. The researcher worked with the transitional coach (TC) who held the role of facilitating the problem-solving along with the management of data collection. The researcher functioned as the resource person (Springer, 2007). Kickett et al. (1986) characterize this as a "bottom-up" orientation because the TC worked with the individuals focusing and recording attention and attentiveness as defined by the participant. Accordingly, it was the TC, who provided the specific parameters, which included the establishment of rapport, explaining the ground rules with the intended purpose to listen, allowing the person time to self-reflect and address social contextual environmental changes and situations that were resulting in problems to which solutions or resolutions were to be considered. The TC facilitated the communication acting as the catalyst, introducing the problem-solving prompts, and recording the participant's defined problem(s), context, and resolutions.

Working Principles. The TC developed professional and personal working- relationships with the participants. Adhering to the ethical standards of a counselor-trained facilitator, confidentiality was maintained. In the presentation of subsequent cases, identifiable information has been removed to maintain the privacy and identity of the participants. Communication is key to this type of research; therefore, the LIBRE Model Ground Rules were used to provide parameters to the exchange (Guerra, 2015):

- Respect—all involved in the problem-solving are held in respect, recognizing that this activity opens the participant to a space of vulnerability.
- Facilitator's role—commitment and responsibility to manage the client's commitment to the problem-solving and the products of the problem-solving exchange.
- Participant safety—the problem-solving is monitored to ensure that the participant does not feel threatened by the standard prompts offered as components of the problem- solving.
- Environmental safety—the location of the problem-solving is critical and the facilitator works with the problem-solver to provide a comfortable and calming backdrop. The participant was given freedom to request the location for problem-solving exchanges to occur; sessions were held at the downtown and main campus, where designated and secure places were identified.
- Confidentiality—problem-solvers are provided confidentiality within the established parameters of the study and participation with the grant.
- Openness—the problem-solvers are encouraged to speak freely within the problem-solving setting. The facilitator listens and records responses to the problem-solving without offering thoughts or opinions to any content presented within the problem-solving exchange.
- Independence—problem-solvers are encouraged to self-regulate; the problem-solving exchange is slowed down to offer the participants as much time as each feels necessary to express the challenge and develop the resolution.

These ground rule standards were shared each time the problem-solving occurred to provide overt participant safeguards to management of the content and context (pp. 42–43).

Agenda. The same agenda and protocol were established for each problem-solving exchange. The first problem-solving exchange occurred as an invitation to

Participants and Research Plan • **47**

participate in the program. Two problem-solving events occurred each semester; however, the participant always had the option to come in to problem-solve at any point within the semester. The problem-solving procedure and prompts were the same with each setting to provide the participants a comfortable and anticipated exchange. With each session, the participant was free to address any content of choice. After the first session, there was the additional revisit of the prior problem-solving generated resolution plans. The participant was invited to speak to actions/non-actions taken to the prior developed LIBRE Model problem-solving plan before entry into the new problem-solving exchange.

Position. The TC presented herself each time in a neutral and nonthreatening position. She welcomed the participant, established rapport by asking questions about how the participant's program was progressing before stepping into the problem-solving exchange. As a trained counselor, she monitored the participant's verbal and nonverbal posture and adjusted herself to maximize the communication.

The TC placed herself in a supportive position with the problem-solvers to situate a shared experience; both persons sat on the same side of the table to process the problem(s). Respected distance was maintained (as the individual moved back away from the table). The intention with the LMSF tool was to draw attention to the problem-solving as an external event, allowing the participant to observe as the facilitator recorded. In essence, the LMSF became a snapshot to the participant and the facilitator as they worked together in the completing of the LMSF and presented challenge.

Rigor. Research is a balance of purpose, process, ethics, and rigor (Springer, 2007). The research must be systematic and rigorous based on trustworthiness checks (Lincoln & Guba, 1985). To this end, credibility, transferability, dependability and confirmability have been addressed. Weekly meetings were held with the transitional coach to review cases and to analyze language, problems, and how each was addressed.

Credibility. As a fundamental element, unless the participants are able to trust the process, they are likely not to commit (Stringer, 2007). Therefore, opportunities were included to allow participants and the TC time to develop a genuine relationship and the level of rapport necessary to explore change and process challenges. The TC also was involved in *observations*. She maintained notes of observed behaviors in other professional development settings and checked-in with participants to inquire their interpretation(s) of those observations. For example, she might be involved in supporting a grant presenter and while in that role, notes that a teacher candidate seemed distracted. She would then make that note so when she had her next meeting with her, she would be able to address the observation. She also worked with the other grant education specialists to acquire additional data to *triangulate* information.

Member checking occurred on a regular basis as the facilitator shared the LMSF data with the problem-solvers. This gave opportunity for the facilitator to

48 • TEACHER CANDIDATE PROBLEM-SOLVING ENGAGEMENT STYLES

clarify and extend the problem-solving experience. At the close of each semester, there was a *participant debriefing* which allowed the participants an opportunity to address the semester's experiences and offer additional information to his/her attention and change patterns. *Diverse case analysis* occurred regularly with the researcher to address the principles of inclusion and to ensure that the process was adhered to in operation. *Referential adequacy* was addressed regularly as concepts and terminology were developed to address the grounded research reflecting the identified theory.

Transferability. The transferability of this research is based on the *detailed description of the process:* each problem-solving exchange has been outlined with parameters and ethical standards for implementation, the *context(s)* and *activities* have protocols that must be followed, and *event* outcomes are tracked according to a detailed procedure (Guerra, 2015). Psychosocial Features are presented and used to summarize participant transitions.

Dependability. An established inquiry audit was developed with a description of the case management procedures. These procedures were followed to provide the basis for judging the extent to which the results were dependable. Additional facilitators were trained and involved in the data collection to create and monitor a dependability to the process, data collection and data analysis.

Confirmability. The established audit trail allows an observer a view of the data collected, instruments, field notes, tapes, journals, or other artifacts related to the study (Guerra, 2015).

SUMMARIZING THOUGHTS

The research design and multi-lens analysis provides the framework for examination of the teacher candidates' complex challenges as presented in preparation, entry into, and professional retention to the field. The systematic problem-solving approach facilitates the examination to challenges confronted. The LIBRE Model cues provided the structure for the exchange. The five open-ended prompts introduce open-ended questions for the participants to address themselves. The goal is to provide the participant a safe space to explore their context and worldviews. The only data collected are the participants' words and expressions. The resultant findings are intended to address the significant problems that face this population as they move into a high turnover profession.

REFERENCES

Baeten, M., & Meeus, W. (2016). Training second-career teachers: A different student profile, a different training approach? *Educational Process: International Journal, 5*(3), 173–201.

Flores, B. B., Claeys, L., & Gist, C. D. (2018). *Crafting culturally efficacious teacher preparation and pedagogies* (pp. 15–24). Lexington Books.

Guerra, N. S. (2009). Illustrations of engagement styles: Four teacher candidates. *Teacher Education & Practice, 22*(1), 95–117.

Guerra, N. S. (2015). *Clinical problem-solving case management*. Rowman & Littlefield and Lexington Books.

Guerra, N. S., Hernandez, A. E., Hector, A., & Crosby, S. (2015). Listen-Identify-Brainstorm-Reality-test-Encourage (LIBRE) model: Addressing special education teacher professional development through a cognitive behavioral approach to teacher induction, *Action in Teacher Education, 34*(4), 334–354.

Holland, C. (2017). Assessing and resolving California's growing teacher shortage. *Teacher College Record.* https://www.tcrecord.org ID Number: 21925.

Jacobson, M. J., Levin, J. A., & Kupur, M. (2019). Education as a complex system: Conceptual and methodological implications. *Educational Researcher, 48*(2), 112–119.

Kickett, D., McCauley, D., & Stringer, E. T. (1986). *Community development processes: An introductory handbook.* Curtin University of Technology.

Lincoln, Y., & Guba, G. M. (1985). *Naturalistic Inquiry.* Sage Publication.

Stringer, E. T. (2004). *Action research.* Pearson Merrill Prentice Hall.

Stringer, E. T. (2007). *Action research* (3rd ed.). Sage Publications.

Stringer, E. T. (2014). *Action research* (4th ed.) Pearson Merrill Prentice Hall.

U. S. Census Bureau. (2010). *State & county quickfacts: Bexar County, TX.* http://quickfacts.census.gov.

UTSA. (2019). *Catalog.* http:utsa.edu/educationhumandevelopment.

CHAPTER 6

CASE STUDY

First Generation Latina Female

INTRODUCTION

Sharon, a twenty-four-year-old Latina female, is married with two children. She describes herself as "blessed." She is a first-generation college student. Sharon lives close to her parents and explains that both her parents and husband are supportive of her continuing her academic study. She is committed to her family and her career development. Sharon grew up in a very conservative Latina family that primarily spoke Spanish at home. She considers herself a bilingual speaker. Sharon is completing a Bachelor of Arts degree while working at the university and states that she has always wanted to be a special education teacher. The idea of an accelerated program sounds perfect, and she is ready to begin this "new adventure." The summer session will begin shortly so Sharon wants to obtain additional information before making her final decision; she meets with the program transitional coach (TC).

The TC explains that the grant-funded accelerated teacher education program involves internship and field experiences that will prepare students for classroom teaching. The TC also explains that there will be academic and transitioning

Teacher Candidate Problem-Solving Engagement Styles:
LIBRE Model Self-Management Analysis, pages 51–72.
Copyright © 2022 by Information Age Publishing
www.infoagepub.com
All rights of reproduction in any form reserved.

51

52 • TEACHER CANDIDATE PROBLEM-SOLVING ENGAGEMENT STYLES

coaches available to provide assistance with professional development. The provided services include strength-based problem solving to assist with anticipated transitions that may occur. The first year of the accelerated study will involve traditional classroom instruction. The second year includes internship and field experience. During this year, the teacher candidates will work side-by-side under an assigned teacher-of-record. The expectation is that these teacher candidates will complete their course work the first year, allowing them to focus on their specialized work to complete the master's degree and teaching certification. The program goal is to provide the participants with the experiences that will make them more marketable, given this focused accelerated work. As part of the interview process, the TC asks her if she would like to participate.

Sharon said "yes" to the invitation to join the teacher accelerated-preparation program and welcomes the opportunities to problem-solve. Her first problem-solving exchange begins with her first summer session immediately upon entry into the program. She has two problem-solving exchanges in the Fall Semester of her first year; followed by two sessions in the Spring Semester. The second year is internship and field experiences. Sharon is working in a school setting; she has two problem-solving exchanges in that Fall Semester and two in the Spring Semester of that second year.

FIRST PROBLEM-SOLVING EXCHANGE

Invitation to Problem-Solve: Considering Graduate School

Sharon is pleased to be offered the opportunity to visit with a transitional coach (TC) and she is ready to problem-solve. The TC welcomes her, and they visit briefly about her BA degree completion and joining the program to seek a master's degree in curriculum and instruction with a certification in special education. Sharon enjoys school and being a student. She is currently working full-time at the university. Sharon is relaxed and comfortable as she speaks with the TC, who asks Sharon if she is ready to problem-solve and the TC explains the ground rules. The TC shows Sharon the graphic LIBRE Model Stick Figure (LMSF) and explains that only her words will be recorded. The TC explains that they will begin at the top of the head of the LMSF. She will offer the prompt, wait for her response, and work down to the feet where any solutions will be recorded along with timelines. Sharon affirms she understands the explanation with a nod, and the TC asks Sharon if she has any additional questions. Sharon responds with "no" and they begin the activity with the TC offering the first prompt.

Beginning here with the hair of your LIBRE Model Stick Figure tool (LMSF), Listen and list challenges you are experiencing." The TC continues to speak and explains that she will record her responses so Sharon may feel free to speak without having to self-reflect, think, talk, and record. Sharon smiles and says, "thanks."

Sharon begins to list her social exchanges as, "finishing her BA (December); my <her> husband is supportive; I <she > have two children; parents are close to

Case Study • 53

me <her> (physically); teaching class at church; works at the university; ready for a change;" and she is a "leadership teacher."

The TC continues; *I can see that you have a lot going on. The next step is to identify the item that you'd most like to process and let's write it as a question.* Sharon states, "How could I devote more time to my son's third grade year?"

Okay, let's now move to the left side of the LMSF and begin brainstorming possible options.

Sharon begins, "(1) Staying less time at my parents; (2) devote specific time on Saturdays in the mornings to study; suggesting here that she dedicate specific time to study (3) practice spelling—faithfully; and (4) driving time—learning is fun." The TC asks if she has any additional thoughts or brainstorm options that she would like to consider; Sharon says, "no." Sharon then decides that she does not want to eliminate any options and the list represents her prioritized order, so they continue.

We now move to the right side of the LMSF to reality-test the prioritized options; what will each of your items look like should you act on each option?

Directly working across her brainstormed options, she continues to further develop her thoughts, "(1) I will feel guilty leaving early; (2) getting up by 10 AM—investment; (3) motivational; and (4) system plan." Sharon is direct with her responses and detailed as she builds on the brainstorming options that she had created for herself.

The TC reviews the LMSF responses and asks Sharon if she is ready to continue. Together they then move to the Encourage prompt.

Encourage—Now as we move to the LMSF feet, we are going to focus on your best plan. It may include some of the information that you have in the above sections; however, it does not necessarily have to include any of that information. It is completely up to you. What do you want to list as your steps to your best solution?

Sharon begins almost as if she is speaking only to herself, "put it in perspective and evaluate options. I will engage Fred and ask for his input." Then continues her presentation to an action statement, "Ask my husband to be involved."

Now let's look at the other foot to identify the timelines for your steps. When will you begin?

Sharon continues, "Tomorrow we can speak—(I'll sell it); will implement Saturday morning first *car time* we can do immediately." This comment seems to indicate a confidence in the relationship with her spouse as she plans to discuss the need and her plan as they drive together in the car; their personal "car time."

Sharon's plan is straightforward with one action planned with a timeline to manage it. Her word of self-encouragement is "activator." The TC and Sharon close the session. Sharon says, "thank you for the time" and concludes by stating that she plans to join the program in the summer (See Figure 6.1 Sharon's First Problem-Solving Exchange).

54 • TEACHER CANDIDATE PROBLEM-SOLVING ENGAGEMENT STYLES

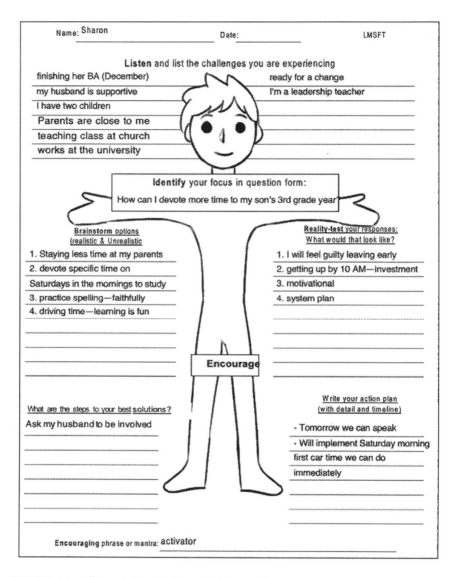

FIGURE 6.1. Sharon's First Problem-Solving Exchange

PROBLEM-SOLVING PSYCHOSOCIAL EXPRESSIONS SUMMARY

The LIBRE Model L—listening prompt provided a platform for Sharon to address her social environment. She was able to identify her focal concern (I –identifying concern question). The B- brainstorming provided her creative space to explore all possible and impossible options and once prioritized she was able to begin thinking about behavioral actions with the R—reality-testing prompt. The importance in noting her psychosocial features and responses to the prompts are to monitor her willingness to self-reflect within the context of her identified social worldview/ecology. The plans are positive and suggest resilience in management.

Sharon is at a pivotal point in her academic career. She has been working and will complete her Bachelor of Arts degree in December. She describes her primary social and cultural community as home: her husband, two children (son and daughter), and her parents. She works at the university, however, that reference to work is only secondary to her primary expressed concern for her son. The primary identity role that she shares is that of "mom." She problem-solves this personal concern with this first exchange. A strong investment is observable in the detailed responses provided to each of the L-I-B-R-E cues. This attentive consistency continued from the beginning to the close of the session.

Engagement Style

Sharon is identified as exhibiting an **actual engagement style,** because of her attentiveness. While in her first problem-solving exchange, several data points were noted: (1) Context—she focused on a personal concern within this first session, (2) Approach—she was attentive in the language used (action-orientated)— actual engagement, (3) Focus—the concern is focused on elements within her control, and (4) Outcome—plan is to immediately involve her husband in assisting their son.

FIRST YEAR SUMMER: SECOND PROBLEM-SOLVING EXCHANGE

Entry into the Accelerated Program

As with the prior meeting, the TC and Sharon speak briefly before beginning the problem-solving exchange. Sharon smiles and updates the TC on how her son is doing. Sharon then indicates that she is ready to begin, and she calmly shares her concerns: "finding an internship in the Fall; being able to graduate on my timeline; helping my son with his reading skills; keeping my husband happy with everything I add in my life; keeping my house clean; and providing enough time for my parents." She stopped and lowered her head as she stared at the LMSF graphic that had been used to record her words. The paper is the focus of her attention; her eyes are on the recorded narrative. She does not look up. The TC asks, "Is that everything?" Sharon nods her head to indicate, "yes."

The TC adjusts the LMSF to allow Sharon a full view to see what has been recorded. Gauging Sharon's openness, the TC pauses allowing Sharon a time to look over the recorded response. After a moment, the TC continues. *The next step is to identify the item that you'd most like to process and let's write it as a question.* The goal with this problem-solving prompt is to work on one expressed challenge.

Sharon replies, "How can I find an internship for the Fall Semester?"

Okay, let's now move to the left side of the LMSF and begin brainstorming possible options.

Sharon is quick to reply, "(1) apply to school districts; (2) prepare myself for an interview; (3) talk to others who have had interviews; (4) go to career services for assistance; (5) search for job postings within school district; and (6) networking."

The TC continues, "anything else?" "Remember we want to consider realistic and non-realistic options." The TC offered Sharon three additional prompting questions with no response before continuing.

We now move to the right side of the LMSF to reality-test. What will each of your items look like? Should you act on each option?

Sharon's demeanor continues to be calm and invested as she provides a behavioral response to each of the brainstormed options, "(1) go to web and fill out applications; (2) read interviewing books/research online; (3) ask students in my cohort who have had interviews; (4) call and make an appointment—request time off; (5) go to web; and (6) mention to everybody that I am looking for a teaching job."

The TC gently moves her finger to the Encourage word written on the LMSF and begins by reviewing the responses that Sharon has offered explaining that she (Sharon) is the one who monitors and manages her next steps. She reassures her that she is in control of herself and that any change she may want to make in terms of how she manages herself will be completely up to her. The TC then offers the next prompt. *Encourage—Now as we move to the LMSF feet, we are going to focus on your best plan. It may include some of the information that you have in the above sections; however, it does not necessarily have to include any of that information. It is completely up to you. What do you want to list as your steps to your best solution?*

Sharon smiles and responds, "Complete three remaining applications; find career services contact and make an appointment to request a mock interview; read interviewing books; go to the web and search for job postings; and continue to network." The TC then resumes. *Now let's look at the other foot to identify the timelines for your steps. When will you begin?*

Sharon is encouraged and says, "I already began yesterday and before Sunday, I will apply to three districts." Then looking up, Sharon continues, "I have my plan. I will contact the career services office to schedule an appointment/mock interview ASAP and continue to network, search for job postings, and read interviewing books." As they closed the session, Sharon indicated that she might have trouble scheduling with career services since she works the same hours that they are open. The TC and Sharon discussed additional options.

Case Study • 57

The TC then asked her to offer herself a word of encouragement which she does as they closed the problem-solving session, "Stay focused, follow your dream, continue working toward your goal and you will conquer it."

Sharon is relaxed and thanked the TC. They set a date for their next meeting in the Fall Semester.

PROBLEM-SOLVING PSYCHOSOCIAL EXPRESSION SUMMARY

The problem-solving timelines are clearly observable. Sharon is now actively involved in graduate school. In a new role as a graduate student, there are challenges that this context introduces. She has already begun to identify them even before the problem- solving begins. The advantage of the LMSF problem-solving exchange is the time-out to see, process, and explore what may have been a nagging feeling for Sharon as she attempted to keep up with her daily changing demands. Her TC describes her as detailed in her thinking and presentation. Sharon had indicated that she had not had the opportunity to attend to self, so she welcomed the exchange. Sharon's data indicates (1) reported role identity—graduate student, (2) context—school, (2) approach—is attentive/actual engagement, and (3) focus— stated as within her control.

The psychosocial expressions suggest that she is working with many new worldview challenges. She is in a new environment as a graduate student and has new personal/professional roles of being a student/teacher candidate. She is concerned about her son and his reading skills; her husband and his happiness; her need for an internship; and spending time with her parents. These identities are being shifted as she identifies her singular challenge, "How can I find an internship for the Fall Semester?" The importance in noting her psychosocial features and the response to the prompts is to monitor her willingness to self-reflect within the context of her identified worldview; she selects to focus on securing a Fall semester internship. The plans are positive and suggest resilience in management.

The following two sections are presented as summaries of the LIBRE Model with the focus on the junctures of Initial and Sustained Attentiveness. Defined, *Initial Attention* is a reflection of the participant's willingness to address social context: Listen and List prompt—attend to the contextual environment, Brainstorm—personal values and cultural beliefs in addressing the identified problem, and Reality-testing—the behavioral considerations associated with acting upon any one brainstormed action. *Sustained Attention* is defined as the willingness to identify a specific concern and follow that identified concern up to the point of developing a resolution plan with detailed timelines. Before moving to the third problem-solving session, this second problem-solving exchange is repeated in the format that will be used for the remaining problem-solving exchanges. The purpose for the repetition is two-fold: (1) to familiarize you with the new format and (2) to highlight her level of attention as expressed across the problem-solving exchange.

58 • TEACHER CANDIDATE PROBLEM-SOLVING ENGAGEMENT STYLES

Initial Attention

Initial attention is designed to welcome and invite the participant to self-reflect. Self-awareness is a prerequisite to self-management; so, the open-ended prompting questions are designed to assist the person to connect with self. Sharon remains attentive throughout this entire opening problem-solving exchange. She brainstorms; however, she only considers realistic options to her identified challenge. Sharon's expressions are focused and intentional. She has no desire to explore unrealistic solutions.

Listen and List. Sharon is quick to share her world. She offers six distinct responses: (1) finding an internship, (2) being able to graduate on the timeline she created, (3) helping her son with his reading skills, (4) keeping her husband happy with everything she is adding to her life, (5) keeping her house clean, and (6) providing enough time for her parents. These unique facets of Sharon's world are expressed as personal and academic concerns. The visual presentation and recording of the challenges offer her an opportunity to see problems as hair on the head of this "stick figure."

Brainstorm. Sharon is open to brainstorm; however, she is only interested in realistic options. She does not judge her solutions; however, she also is not willing to explore other non-realistic options. While this prompt is stated to generate numerous options that are both realistic and not realistic, Sharon has selected to offer only realistic considerations. And given her presentation, the TC is left to wonder if this is a characteristic that Sharon maintains in problem solving. Sharon is attentive to the problem solving and to herself and she is observed as pressing forward to explore all of her generated solutions.

Reality-Test. Sharon offers additional information when asked to reality-test. This time she explains in greater detail what behavioral actions will be required. For example, "go to web and fill out applications." The TC scribes all of the information as Sharon dictates. Once Sharon has stepped through her six options, they move forward.

Sharon remains visibly attentive to her identified challenge and exploration of solutions.

Sustained Attention

There are distinct attentiveness skills required to create a goal and to maintain the attentive investment to complete it. Sustained attention in problem solving is observable as a series of self-motivated, managed, and unrelenting investments. Sharon is observed identifying a specific challenge/goal within her control and as she processed that goal, she maintained that singular attentive investment.

Identify a Challenge. Sharon is open to identifying a specific challenge within her control. In addressing sustained attention, this suggests that she is an indicator of her remaining attentiveness to herself and her role in problem-solving the concern she has identified. The specificity of the concern becomes the goal for

Case Study • 59

continued motivated investment. Sharon is clear in the statement of intention for this investment; "How can I find an internship for the Fall Semester?"

Encourage. The two sub-skills of the engagement step are designed to note the distinctions between what "needs to be done" as compared to the "accountability in completion." In Sharon's case, she has streamlined her investment.

Best steps solution. Sharon's what "needs to be done" steps include— "complete three remaining applications; find career services to contend with and make an appointment for a mock interview; read interviewing books; go to web and search for job posting; and to continue to network." These are Sharon's intended actions.

Timeline. Goal orientation planning includes specificity and invested attention statements; "accountability in completion." Sharon explains her plan, "Yesterday" and continues, "Before Sunday, apply to three districts."

Engagement Style

Sharon, as a teacher candidate, provides an example of what many students experience as they come into a new environment with new challenges and expectations. Sharon was aware of her challenges, and to keep up with all the changes, she created a priority in what first must be addressed. Sharon is exhibiting an **actual engagement style** with her self-managed approach which appears to be motivating and contributing to her relief. The opportunity to work with the TC provided her "space" to self-reflect and to re-examine her plan. She was quick to develop an action plan.

Subsequent problem-solving exchanges are presented with the similar Initial and Sustained Attention narrative patterns that articulate the data collected. Table 6.1 displays: (1) Defined Identity—student; context of the problem identified— school oriented, (2) approach—invested; actual engagement, and (3) focus— within her control, assuming responsibility for elements she could control.

FIRST YEAR FALL SEMESTER: THIRD EXCHANGE

Developing a Self-Managed Investment toward Self-Regulation

The TC welcomes Sharon and asks her how her plan went. Sharon is quick to report that she is working at her internship site. Sharon asks if they may begin their problem solving because there is something that she would like her (TC) to assist her with. The TC's response is, "of course." They begin.

Initial Attention

Sharon presents herself with a similar attentiveness to their prior problem-solving exchange. This time, however, her focus is not on school. There is a heightened sense of urgency in addressing her personal needs. Ground rules are reviewed, and the TC presents a blank LMSF form. Sharon smiles and they begin.

60 • TEACHER CANDIDATE PROBLEM-SOLVING ENGAGEMENT STYLES

Listen. The TC offers, *beginning here with the hair of your LMSF, Listen and list all that is happening. Any concerns.*

Sharon reports, "New position; kids are back to school; Mom is sick; homework is overwhelming; and trying to keep marriage stable." The TC prompts two additional times and Sharon indicates that this is all, and they continue. Sharon's focus is, "How do I dedicate a little more time to my marriage?" Sharon is ready to move into the brainstorming prompt.

Brainstorm. Much like with Sharon's first visit, she is direct and does not want to explore unrealistic options. She begins, "set aside a timeframe on my calendar; planning activities for the kids; finding activities so that we can spend time together." As before, Sharon offers no unrealistic considerations, and her prioritizing follows the order she stated so they move to the reality-testing prompt.

Reality-Test. Her behavioral thought, as presented, is to, "set aside lunch with husband one day a week; arrange with work schedules. Find something both children would like and use that time to spend with husband. Join husband for Saturday bike rides. Plan date nights when we can go dining, movies, coffee and/or dinner." The TC follows Sharon's explanation. Together they review Sharon's exchange before moving to the Encourage prompt.

Sustained Attention

Sharon is invested and motivated. She is not afraid to change. She is decisive and once she is certain of a direction, she is ready to move forward.

Identify a Challenge. When invited to indicate her focal concern, she said, "How do I dedicate a little more time to my marriage?" The goal is specific, within her control, and clearly articulated.

Encourage. The encourage step is designed to summarize, motivate, and affirm investment. Sharon is self-managing and invested so she was ready to address her best steps.

Best steps solution. Sharon is immediate in her response. "Talk with my husband and see what the best day is to have lunch with him; talk with work and see when I can take a lunch; sit down with children and see what they would like to do; see if we can afford it, then schedule one day I'm not at school (Monday or Friday); have determination to bike with husband—quality time; set up a monthly date night." She smiles and awaits the next prompt.

Timeline. Sharon indicates that she is going to take action immediately, "as soon as this afternoon—talk with husband. Start researching children's activities this weekend and next week; could easily start to schedule monthly date nights today—sit down with calendar and husband." And in reference to her plan, she indicates that she is going to be up by 12:00 A.M., Sharon explains, "beginning Wednesday."

No word of self-encouragement is offered; only the appreciation for the meeting and leaving with her mission in hand. The TC reports that Sharon was calm and showed appropriate affect. She was talkative and responsive.

Case Study • 61

Engagement Style

Sharon makes a subtle change in her self-management focus, but her engagement style remains the same as it was with her first exchange. Her first session investment addressed her larger "work worldview" context—school and academic expectations. This session, she came in with identified challenges in the home more than at school and her urgency was in addressing a personal identified need. Once more attentive, she was ready to dialog how best to address her concern; "dedicate more time to marriage." She needed to figure out how to create a plan that is direct and specific. "Talk with <my> husband and see what the best day is to have lunch with him," and when, "this afternoon." She also is thinking about her children as she plans to, "sit down with children <to> see what they would like to do," and when, "this weekend and next." Sharon's **Actual engagement style** appears to be an approach she is comfortable implementing in working toward a solution. Her sustained attentiveness appears to motivate her to go forward with her plan. She had constructed a self-managed plan with a self-regulated solution. The plan is within her control; the family's response to the plan is not.

FIRST YEAR FALL SEMESTER / FOURTH EXCHANGE

Processing New and Complex Spaces

The semester has passed quickly. Sharon has requested this visit because she is struggling with what to do now that the semester is ending. The TC and Sharon agree on a time and date and begin their visit. The TC inquiries about how her last plan went and she reports some change has occurred. Sharon indicates that all is going well, however, she is most interested in talking about the end of the semester. The TC nods her head and presents a blank LMSF so that they may begin their work together. The TC re-states the ground rules, Sharon smiles as she listens. Because she is familiar with the process, she patiently waits for the TC's explanation. When asked if she has any questions, she replies "no" and they begin.

Initial Attention

Sharon is comfortable with the LIBRE Model problem solving. She is anticipating the opportunity to share with TC exactly where she is within the semester. Final examinations are occurring soon, and she is feeling the stress of the season.

Listen. Sharon begins to list, "finish finals tonight; prepare for family coming; and get ready for Christmas." The TC affirms that she does have much on her plate. She asks Sharon to identify a concern. The focused question she presents is, "How do I have the Christmas presents under the tree by the 24th?"

Brainstorm. As they begin the brainstorming, the TC offers the prompt as she has before with the prior two exchanges. This time Sharon's immediate with her responses: "go shopping; make a list; set the budget; shop online; get ads from Sunday paper." The TC asks if there are any other options that they might want to

62 • TEACHER CANDIDATE PROBLEM-SOLVING ENGAGEMENT STYLES

consider; Sharon's response is only to shake her head to indicate no. The TC asks if she wants to eliminate any. Sharon states, "I'm not shopping online and not going to get ads from the Sunday paper."

Reality-Test. As they begin to address this next prompt, Sharon states: "On Saturday—go out; list persons and gift ideas; talk with husband—decide on amounts." No other considerations were offered.

Sustained Attention

Sharon's sustained attention is a continued investment expressed in a specific and detailed presentation. **Identify a Challenge.** Sharon explains that she is "struggling, "How do I have the Christmas presents under the tree by the 24th?"

Encourage. The TC reviews Sharon's presentation beginning from her opening statement up to this final Encourage prompt.

Best steps solution. Familiar with the prompts, Sharon continues, "I need to set a budget, make list, take mother-in-law with me on Saturday, get pedicure or manicure to reward my shopping." She then indicates her timeline.

Timeline. "Friday night—set budget; Friday night—make list; Saturday—take mother-in-law; Saturday—get pedicure or manicure." When asked for a word of encouragement, her only response was, "pedicure/manicure."

Engagement Style

Sharon provides a different engagement style with this exchange. She is invested in only one action—"getting ready for Christmas." The TC reports that she is relaxed as she explains that she will be finishing her "last final tonight." The details are focused on preparing for the family that will be coming in and getting ready for Christmas. She was actively invested with a great deal of attention to the upcoming Christmas need, "presents under the tree." The data collected includes (1) context of the problem solving is "Christmas," (2) the approach is that of a **goal-focused engagement style**, and (3) focus—self; "How do I have the Christmas presents under the tree by the 24th?"

FIRST YEAR SPRING SEMESTER/
FIRST SESSION: FIFTH EXCHANGE

Sharon has now been in graduate school for two semesters (summer and fall); she is beginning her Spring Semester. She meets with the TC in February, one month after classes began. The TC welcomes her; they chat and then Sharon indicates that she is ready. The ground rules are reviewed, and the first prompt is offered.

Case Study • **63**

Initial Attention

Sharon lists, "Valentine's Day planning; daughter is sick; work—considering whether to apply for new promotion; behind on school reading; and husband's moods—medication coming."

The next step is to identify the item that you'd most like to process and let's write it as a question. Sharon states, "How can I organize my time for schoolwork?"

Okay, let's now move to the left side of the LMSF and begin brainstorming possible options.

Sharon begins, "quit my job; take my lunch break to read my chapters; go to first service on Sundays instead of second; on Wednesdays go to Barnes & Noble; on Saturdays –study; use Saturday afternoon for special projects test." Sharon only eliminates one of her brainstormed options that of "quit my job" and indicated that her priority to those that remain are exactly as they are listed.

We now move to the right side of the LMSF to reality-test; what will each of your items look like should you act upon each option?

Sharon continues, "read some pages while eating; get out of church by 11—use extra hours to read from 12:00 pm to 5:00 pm; from 8:00 pm to 12:00 am—leave the house to focus on ABA material. Make sure not to stay up too late the night before; and ask sister to help with parents in those times."

Sustained Attention

Sharon has been focused from the beginning of her problem-solving experience. Sharon clearly stated her challenge and goal, "How can I organize my time for schoolwork?"

The *Encourage* prompt—*Now let's move to the LMSF feet, the focus on your best plan. It may include some of the information that you have in the above sections; however, it does not necessarily have to include any of that information. It is completely up to you. What do you want to list as your steps to your best solution?*

Sharon quickly responds, "go back to work—open calendar with those times; go to husband's calendar and block those times; implement new schedule times all at once; and talk with family about these changes."

Now let's look at the other foot to identify the timelines for your steps. When will you begin?

Sharon returns to her plan and asks the TC to draw arrows from each step to the timeline—go back to work—open calendar with those times → today; go to husband's calendar and block those times → today; implement new schedule times all at once → Wednesday (going to Barnes & Noble); and talk with family about these changes → Thursday."

64 • TEACHER CANDIDATE PROBLEM-SOLVING ENGAGEMENT STYLES

Sharon's mantra is stated confidently as self-talk to encourage this aggressive plan; "this is only three months—then I'll be two classes away from finishing coursework."

Engagement Style

Sharon's problem-solving attentiveness is again attentive with an **actual engagement style**. The one observed exception was at the end-of-semester "gifts under the tree," which was a singular goal-focused engagement. It is not surprising that her attention is now more directed to finishing her work with an increased investment and her encouragement is with the end in sight. The TC reports that Sharon is overwhelmed in her tone and demeanor. Sharon reports that she had a lot on her mind, and she is feeling pulled in many directions. The data provided here was (1) context—finishing her degree; (2) approach—actual engagement; and (3) focus—managing her time for increased study; areas all within her control. Sharon is once more assuming an **actual engagement style**.

FIRST YEAR SPRING SEMESTER/
SECOND SESSION: SIXTH EXCHANGE

Sharon's last semester is busy. She is continuing to live in a reported state of stress and as such is ready to problem-solve and share her current situation. Once the ground rules are reviewed, the initial **Listen and List** prompt is offered.

Initial Attention

Sharon begins, "finals and research paper; trip to Puerto Rico; ABA paper; project at work" and closes by saying, "I am sick." Sharon then continues as she references the second prompt of I-identifying a focus, "How can I prepare myself for finals to feel ready and remove stress from my shoulders?

Sharon continues without waiting for the external **Brainstorming** prompt to be offered, she continues, "take time off to prepare; work all weekend on it; organize my weekend and next week and schedule my time ahead of time." She then closes by stating, "do not study and forget about all." Then immediately deletes that one final option. As before, she indicates that her list represents her priorities, so they continue.

Sharon's **Reality-testing** continues as she explains the implications of her brainstormed options, "take time off to prepare—need to talk to boss for time off; work all weekend on it—family will feel neglected"; then closes by stating, "organize my weekend and next week and schedule my time ahead of time—this could work if I talk to my family and explain what I need to do."

Case Study • **65**

Sustained Attention

Sharon's **I-identified concern** was stated as a question, which read, "How can I prepare myself for finals to feel ready and remove stress from by shoulders? She appears to be referencing the LMSF with reference to the shoulders. The graphic organizer has the problem-solver place the identified challenge on the shoulders and sometimes this location is in reference to explaining how an unaddressed problem can weigh you down as shoulder pressure.

Sharon's final **Encourage** prompt finds the same attentiveness. Sharon explains her plan, "divide my work and prioritize it → talk to my family about my need to be prepared for finals; work on one test at a time, prepare study guide → organize my ideas and work, take the research methods (RM) material first, then the ABA material, and prepare study guide; explain this to my family, this is finals week and I need more time to study → schedule in my calendar that Monday and Tuesday I will prepare and study for RM then Wednesday, Thursday, and Friday I will study for ABA and will have the weekend to review it all."

After concluding her plan with timelines, she closes with self-statement review, "this semester was hard and long but I am almost done. I know I can do it and I will be fine." Sharon's context—school; her approach—actual engagement; and her focus on what she can control—herself.

PROBLEM-SOLVING PSYCHOSOCIAL EXPRESSION SUMMARY

The timeliness of the problem solving is clearly observable with this teacher candidate. She has now completed her graduate school in-class requirements. The second year of this accelerated program involves working in the school for internship. This last problem-solving exchange suggests a confidence in her student role and as the end of the semester challenges arose, she was ready to identify her problem-solving plan. The advantage of the LMSF problem-solving exchange is the time-out to reflect, process, and explore what Sharon may have been experiencing and the "pull away time" allows her to keep up with her daily changing demands. Sharon's problem-solving data indicates that (1) context—her focus school, (2) approach—is attentive and exhibiting an **actual engagement style**, and (3) focus—is within her control.

SECOND YEAR FALL SEMESTER/
FIRST SESSION: SEVENTH EXCHANGE

The second year of this accelerated teacher education program occurs in the schools as a series of internship experiences. The goal is to acclimate the teacher candidate to the culture and day-to-day work experience. The teacher candidates work side-by-side with the teachers that they are assigned to work with over the course of the semester. This presents a unique experience for the students; now, rather than being able to regulate their daily investment, they must work under the leadership and direction of their assigned teacher.

66 • TEACHER CANDIDATE PROBLEM-SOLVING ENGAGEMENT STYLES

Working in the Classroom under an Assigned Teacher

Sharon is now working with a special education teacher and a regular education teacher. She is aware that as a special education teacher, she will likely be working with this type of teaching configuration. She is learning about her profession outside the university classroom. In school, she was taught that she would be assisting the regular education teacher in creating modification for students' identified needs. This is what she expected to see once she was in the public-school classroom. This model was not what she found when she was assigned to the fourth grade where she was told that she would be working with the special education and regular education teachers.

Initial Attention

The TC welcomes Sharon who feels like she and the TC have already been through so much together. Sharon asks the TC if they may begin; to which the TC immediately responds, "of course." The ground rules and first response are offered, **Listen and list**, "what would you like to share today?"

Sharon begins, "balancing everything; learning everything by myself; special education teacher plus regular teacher responsibilities; creating lesson plans ahead of time; paperwork; 70-hour week working; and <Annual Review and Dismissal Meeting> ARD." She then followed up with her **Identified concern**, "How can I prepare my lesson plans ahead of time?"

Sharon is familiar with the problem-solving process, so the dialog from **Brainstorming** to the **Reality-testing** is moved along without any hesitation. The TC reports that Sharon appears frustrated and Sharon reports feeling like the work demands, stress, and responsibilities are falling directly on her.

Sharon brainstorms, "teachers have not been creating their lessons ahead of time; use fourth grade teachers' plans as they copy ahead of time; use internet handouts; use resource I found in the closet; education specialist." The TC asks if there are any options that she would like to eliminate and Sharon says, "yes" then continues, "Use Internet handouts." The TC asks Sharon to prioritize the remaining options and Sharon states that she would like to keep the remaining options in the order that they have been identified so the TC asks Sharon to reality-test. Sharon immediately continues, "(1) teachers have not been creating their lessons ahead of time → so I cannot modify my plans ahead of time; (2) use fourth grade teachers' plans as they copy ahead of time → copy—start tomorrow, pick one day to modify 3:00–8:00 pm, put in binders by days, research; (3) resources I found in closet → use activities—I don't have time to go through it all; (4) education specialist → contact Sarah."

Sustained Attention

Sharon stopped right there. She went on to explain that she did not feel like the teachers she was working with were doing their jobs and as a result she was

Case Study • 67

unable to complete hers. She felt overwhelmed and not supported. Sharon said that she was stressed. She went on to say that she had very little time for herself and her family. Sharon did acknowledge, looking back, that she was "now getting faster at completing the school documentation, but the process is still time consuming." And she closed by saying that "the university faculty would be going by the following day to evaluate how things have been going."

Engagement Style

Sharon exhibited a classic **Venting Engagement Style**. She explained in detail what was occurring in her immediate world and how it was impacting her directly and indirectly as she shared that she is unable to spend time with her family. In the true nature of venting, a venter vents about what is not under their control because they are unable to control what is occurring; the best they can do is invest in telling the story and the frustration of feeling that it is all out of their control.

There is a healthy side to Sharon's venting; first, she is venting in a safe space that will not affect the workplace, and second, given the provided confidentiality, she is taking time to reflect about how she is feeling without drawing others into the narrative. It is also interesting to note that Sharon is now feeling comfortable to be able to vent about what is occurring. The data collected from this session: context—internship in the school, approach—venting engagement style with the recognition that she is limited in what is within her control, and focus—not to act, rather, only to express strong feelings about the current situation.

SECOND YEAR FALL SEMESTER/ SECOND SESSION: EIGHTH EXCHANGE

Sharon is now in her final semester. She is both stressed and anticipatory as she prepares herself for graduation and her new profession as a special education teacher.

Initial Attention

Salutations are exchanged and Sharon is ready to begin. The **Listen and List** challenges prompt is offered, and Sharon begins to list, "finishing papers / projects for internship class (3 out of 5); fix book report into summary for website; final; creating a website for class—finding time to sit down and do it; and car is broken down."

Sharon creates an **Identified concern** of "How can I find time to complete everything for my internship class?" Then immediately continues with **Brainstorming** options that address the stated concern. They read: "I'm not going to do it; take a day off; use the weekend of the 15th; finish everything left; utilize Sarah at school; manage my time; use support; and checklists." Once she finishes the brainstorming, Sharon is ready to reflect on those generated options. She strikes off the first two and indicates that she would like to keep the priorities as they

68 • TEACHER CANDIDATE PROBLEM-SOLVING ENGAGEMENT STYLES

are listed. She then moves to the **Reality-testing**, which is extended behavioral thought to the generated options: "(1) use the weekend of the 15th → I care about my GPA too much; I am still in a probation period at work and the weekend of the 15th is my son's birthday; (2) finish everything left over during Thanksgiving break; (3) utilize Sarah at school → she is giving me ideas; (4) manage my time; support → from my family, and (5) use checklists → go back to this system."

Sustained Attention

Sharon's **Identified concern** of "How can I find time to complete everything for my internship class?" sets the tone for her problem solving and continued investment. While it is not as detailed as prior sessions, the identified challenge remains within her control. As Sharon moves forward to the Encourage prompt, she has three specific steps which she lists as: "(1) work during scheduled time → next weekend; (2) organize and manage my time → this week and over next few weeks; and (3) develop checklists again to motivate me to complete things → soon." Her self-stated mantra, "God is in Control."

Engagement Style

Sharon has returned to an **actual engagement style**, a preference engagement style given the frequency of its use. She again identified a concern within her control, however, this time it was not as specific as with her prior identified challenges. The TC indicates that Sharon is a little more detached; however, she is attentive up to the close of the session. Sharon reports that she has much to do and little time to accomplish everything. Sharon does also indicate that "things are getting better" and she is completing her job in a timelier manner with the more experience she has. Sharon admits, "it is hard adjusting from a job where I was close to perfect to this current teaching position where I do not know how to do everything perfectly since I am still new." Sharon then admitted that is not realistic thinking for her and that she is trying to be more realistic with her expectations for herself. She states that her husband also helps her and indicated that she has feelings of a lack of control combined with high levels of responsibility for her job. Sharon concludes by stating that simply staying to herself and staying out of the teachers' "venting" lounge is what she needs to do and with that indicated, she feels "isolated." However, that is the best way to function in her current position.

THIRD YEAR FALL SEMESTER/
FIRST SESSION: NINTH EXCHANGE

Sharon has graduated. She has selected to come back in to problem-solve. The TC welcomes her, and they visit briefly before they begin their session. Sharon is now working as a special education teacher, but she does not want to talk about work.

Case Study • 69

Initial Attention

Ground rules are reviewed, and the first **Listen and List** prompt is offered. Sharon is ready, "getting used to new software Annual Review Dismissal (ARDs); handling behaviors in the classroom; and son starting middle school." Her focused concern comes even as the **Identify a Concern** prompt is offered, "How can I adjust to my son being in middle school?"

Sharon **Brainstorms**, "he has more homework; and he is involved in more activities." She continues with her **Reality-testing**, "I am a chauffeur but at least I don't stay so late at work." Her responses suggest that she is not even ready to address the question concern she created.

Sustained Attention

Her question of, "How can I adjust to my son being in middle school?" has not yet been addressed. While the question as it is stated is within her control, she has yet to be able to bring herself to identifying how she will adjust to her son being in middle school. With the Encourage prompt offered, her only response is "I will continue to support my son as he transitions into middle school." Her mantra, "I am blessed!" The TC and Sharon talk further, and Sharon explains that work is going well. She is completing her job tasks "much quicker this year versus last year and she is feeling good about this." Sharon went on to say that she is adjusting to the demands of her special education classroom." Her concern is her son and assisting him transitioning into middle school this year, which takes her back to her mantra as she explains, "I need to lean on my faith to help cope with the stressors."

Engagement Style

Sharon recognizes that with her son growing older, she is limited. The problem-solving addresses her personal reflections and helplessness. Sharon has exhibited a **Potential Engagement Style**; this is suggestive of someone that is really not ready to engage or for whatever reason is selecting not to engage. This is the first time that Sharon has assumed this non-action oriented passive position. However, even in this self-regulated space she is reflective and reports self as "Blessed."

THIRD YEAR SPRING SEMESTER/
FIRST SESSION: TENTH EXCHANGE

Last meeting with Sharon, she is completing her second semester as a first-year special education teacher-of-record.

Initial Attention

She is busy in her work as a special education teacher. After visiting with the TC, she asks if they may begin the problem solving. Ground rules and the first

Listen and List prompt is offered, and Sharon begins, "comps; sleep but wake up thinking about what I need to do; overwhelmed with job; TAKS; and meeting with teacher and principal." She responds quickly to the **Identify a concern** prompt as she states, "How do I prepare to present my point of view to the principal and other teacher?" **Brainstorming** she begins, "research to find support for my decision with this student; pull the student's data; take time to relax this weekend; and go to TEA website." Without eliminating any of the options and using the list as her prioritized list, she continues: "research to find support for my decision with this student → Google; pull the student's data → show what the needs are and examine objectives; take time to relax this weekend → sleep in tomorrow and take a hot bath; and go to TEA website → search for fifth grade study guide to explain myself."

Sustained Attention

Sharon's attention is maintained to her **Identified Concern**, "How do I prepare to present my point of view to the principal and other teacher?" Similar to her prior problem-solving experiences, Sharon is specific and clear with her plan and timelines which include: "(1) use TEA materials to prove what I am doing with student → weekend; (2) find examples → Monday; and (3) do lesson plans for next week and use as examples → over the weekend.

Engagement Style

Sharon is once more exhibiting an **Actual Engagement Style** in her approach to this identified challenge. Her reflections are detailed, and focus is consistent as she considers creating change. The action orientation reflects her attention to the problem and to the resolution.

BRINGING THE PROBLEM-SOLVING EVENTS TOGETHER

Problem-Solving Psychosocial Expression Summary

Sharon came in as a first-generation student who completed her Bachelor of Arts degree, but with the desire to become a special education teacher. She reported having a supportive family, however, over the course of this time she also recognized the impact of her schooling and work investment. She made specific shifts to attend to her husband and son. While she had a preference to being action-oriented, she also recognized that sometimes, action is not the best solution in handling challenges.

Engagement Styles in Review

Sharon had a defined preference toward an Actual Engagement Style. There were however, three times when she shifted her problem-solving approach. The first observed change was with the pressure of Christmas at the close of her school

Case Study • 71

TABLE 6.1. Sharon's Problem Solving Data Narrative

Problem-Solving Session	Identity/Context	Problem Solving Approach	Challenge Focus
First Session: Interview for the Program	Parent/Family	Actual Engagement Style	How could I devote more time to my son's third grade year?/ Within her control
Second Session: Spring First Semester	Student/School	Actual Engagement Style	How can I find an internship for the Fall? / Within her control
Third Session: Spring First Semester	Wife/Family	Actual Engagement Style	How do I dedicate a little more time to my marriage? / Within her control
Fourth Session: Spring First Semester	Parent/Family	Goal-focused Engagement Style	How do I have the Christmas presents under the tree by the 24th?/Within her control
Fifth Session: Fall Second Semester	Student/School	Actual Engagement Style	How can I organize my time for schoolwork?/Within her control
Sixth Session: Fall Second Semester	Student/School	Actual Engagement Style	How can I prepare myself for finals to feel ready and remove stress from my shoulders?/ Within her control
Seventh Session: Fall Second Semester	Student/School	Venting Engagement Style	How can I prepare my lesson plans ahead of time?/Not within her control
Eighth Session: Fall Second Semester	Student/School	Actual Engagement Style	How can I find time to complete everything for my internship class?/Within her control
Ninth Session: Spring Third Semester	Parent/Family	Potential Engagement Style	How can I adjust to my son being in middle school?/Within her control
Tenth Session: Spring Third Semester	Student/School	Actual Engagement Style	How to prepare to present my point of view to the principal and other teacher?/Within her control

semester. She became Goal-focused to meet a specific defined need without addressing anything but that specific need. The second time was when she began her internship experience; she realized that she was not in control. She shifted her engagement style to accommodate what she was experiencing with the social context of the school setting. Her response was to visit the TC and within the safety of that setting process the stress and frustration she was experiencing. Sharon exhibited a Venting Engagement Style.

With that resolution addressed, she returned to her preferred Actual Engagement Style. She continued with this engagement preference until the challenge of

72 • TEACHER CANDIDATE PROBLEM-SOLVING ENGAGEMENT STYLES

her son moving into middle school, this third time she expressed helplessness and avoided processing her concern; she assumed a Potential Engagement Style. She concluded by reframing the challenge as a blessing.

Each of the Engagement Styles met a need. The Actual Engagement Style motivated Sharon to action; the Goal-focused Engagement Style zeroed in on what had to be accomplished without external extenuating context, and the Venting Engagement Style provided Sharon an opportunity to just "blow off steam." Finally, the Potential Engagement Style was a non-investment response. She recognized that she did not have control so there was no action for her to assume that would change the situation. Her son was going into middle school.

SUMMARY

Sharon experienced numerous challenges with her transition from student to teacher. While she attempted to anticipate what this program would require and how she would manage herself and her family, she found that there were times when she was unable or not prepared to transition. The problem-solving venue provided her a safety outlet for managing the anticipated and more importantly, the unanticipated events.

The focus on attention patterns allowed the opportunity to identify engagement styles that "fit" her stated identity and context. There are positive and negative features to each engagement style. When the engagement style is matched to the appropriate setting, the participant can remain resilient in self-management even under stressful conditions. The TC provided her relational support that allowed her to transition across the multiple identity roles that she experienced over this time. Sharon provided a picture of a personalized transition—adjusting engagement styles—to meet multiple identities and contextual needs. When she knew she had no control, she vented to release the frustration of not being in control. The positive was that she went to the TC who held that relational support without judgment. This afforded her the freedom to express herself without injury to herself or anyone else.

CHAPTER 7

CASE STUDY OF A MALE

Multicultural

INTRODUCTION

Harry is a thirty-four-year-old male. His mother is White, and his father, Latino. Harry lives within and across these two cultures. He indicates that he wishes he had been able to better understand his father's culture; however, his father was always away working. Harry is now married, and his wife is White Anglo Saxon. He reports that family is very important to him, and that as an adult male, he plans to spend as much time as he can with his wife and child. Harry has completed his Bachelor of Science degree as a civil engineer. He worked at a local bank after graduation, and it was here that he met his wife. He describes himself as a rural person; he loves the country and enjoys the freedom of living in the open space. After marrying, he and his wife began renting a farm. While she was not in favor of this country move, she wants to support him. When he indicated that he wanted to return to college to focus on his real aspiration of becoming a math teacher, she encouraged him and suggested that he quit his job to participate in classes full-time. He indicates that he considers himself fortunate to have achieved one degree and is excited to now address what he believes is his true calling. He aspires to be a math teacher.

Teacher Candidate Problem-Solving Engagement Styles:
LIBRE Model Self-Management Analysis, pages 73–88.
Copyright © 2022 by Information Age Publishing
www.infoagepub.com
All rights of reproduction in any form reserved.

73

74 • TEACHER CANDIDATE PROBLEM-SOLVING ENGAGEMENT STYLES

FIRST SESSION: INTERVIEW

Invitation to Problem-Solve: Considering Graduate School

The Transitional Coach (TC) introduced herself to Harry and explained that the overall program was to support the teacher candidates as they transitioned through their master's degree into their desired teaching profession. Together they reviewed the resources that would be available to him. She explained her role in assisting with strength-based problem solving and facilitating the series of transitions that he would likely experience. She closed by reviewing the accelerated master's program curriculum that included the course work that would prepare him for the certification exam, a state requirement in becoming a math teacher. Harry was open and willing to explore the problem-solving resource. He mentioned that he has been financially making a "good living" for his family, so with the invitation to problem-solve, he agreed and selected "work—financial" implications as his focal concern. Harry said that he was ready to begin the program and welcomed the opportunity to problem-solve. The TC explained the LIBRE Model, the LIBRE Model ground rules, and how the LIBRE Model Stick Figure (LMSF) would be used to record each of his problem-solving sessions. Harry said he was fine and ready to try-out the problem-solving support.

Initial Attention

The TC provided the first **Listen and List** prompt to Harry who in response began to list his concerns while the TC recorded each. She positioned the LMSF form so that he could see what she was writing, and she emphasized that she would record only his words.

Harry identified his "wife, child, family, and job" as his environmental/social contextual concerns. The TC then provided the second prompt. **Identify your focus** and state it as a question? Harry's response, "taking time off from work—financially."

The TC then invited Harry to **Brainstorm** possible solutions to his stated concern. His responses included: "saving, cutting back, and family." When asked if he wanted to eliminate any of his brainstormed options, he shook his head to indicate "no." The TC then asked him to *prioritize his options* and he stated that he was comfortable with his next step direction in processing each.

They then proceeded to the **Reality-testing**, which includes his imagining behaviorally playing out each option and explaining what it would look like if he did move forward with each. Harry asked the TC to extend the lines from the brainstorming to the reality-testing section. His presentation followed: "(1) saving → saving account; cutting back → across the board; and family → if need be."

Sustained Attention

The TC takes a moment to review his work and explains that up to this point, there has not been a request to create any action or to explore any change com-

Case Study of a Male • 75

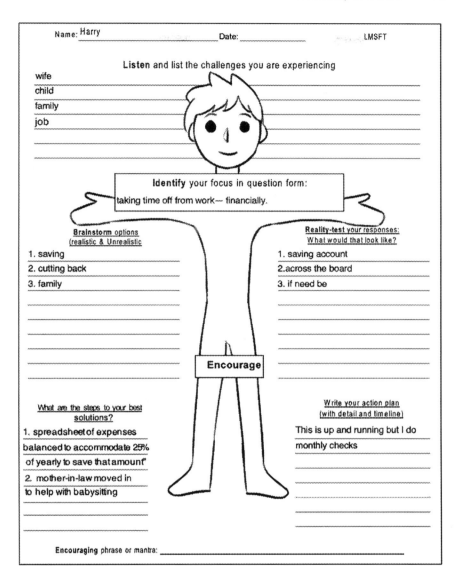

FIGURE 7.1. Harry's First Problem-Solving Exchange

mitment. Harry nods his head in agreement as she continues. The time and space up to this point has been explorative and reflective. His thoughts are about the identified concern. The TC then indicates that she would like him to consider creating a plan of action that would address his identified concern. The TC asked if he was ready and Harry said, "yes." While Harry's response to the **Identify your**

focus and state it as a question did not occur as a question, it remained as Harry's response, "taking time off from work—financially."

The TC then offers the **Encourage** prompt that includes creating a ***Best Steps Plan*** and ***Timeline*** for completion of each step to assist with accountability. Harry receives the prompt and begins explaining that he has created a: "spreadsheet of expenses balanced to accommodate 25% of yearly to save that amount" and <his> mother-in-law moved in to help with babysitting." When asked about timelines, the response was simply, "this is up and running but I do monthly checks" (See Figure 7.1 Harry's First Problem-Solving Exchange).

PROBLEM-SOLVING PSYCHOSOCIAL EXPRESSIONS SUMMARY

Harry welcomed the opportunity to talk about his worldview context consisting of family and potential challenges that may occur with his changing professions; however, he also expressed that he had made the necessary changes that would occur. Thus, this problem-solving session was observed as reflective rather than action oriented. His engagement is **potential**. Harry stated that he knew that there would be financial changes, however, he also indicates that his calculations have been completed and supported so that he should now just continue to monitor his prepared spreadsheets.

Engagement Style

A **Potential Engagement Style** is reflective; it is a filtered approach to problem solving. In Harry's case, he reports on what he has already implemented. He already considered the anticipated financial changes that will need to occur now that he is no longer a banker and adjusted as needed; thus, he only reports what he has already decided.

FIRST YEAR FIRST SEMESTER: SECOND SESSION: CAREER CONSEQUENCE CONSIDERATIONS

Initial Attention

Harry has now joined the program and is taking a full course load as a graduate student. He welcomes the opportunity to meet with the TC. They chat briefly before beginning the session. She offers the ground rules and shares the blank LMSF so that he is able to observe every word that is recorded. The TC offers the first prompt, "**Listen and List** challenges you are experiencing."

Harry reports, "Financial, changing careers from civil engineer to teacher." The TC offers a prompt, but when Harry shakes his head to indicate that he has nothing else to share, she then offers the second prompt, "**Identify your focus** in a question form." Harry's focus, "How will I pay bills?"

The **Brainstorm** prompt is offered; Harry responds with, "savings; plan for future; and win the lottery." He smiles, and when asked to prioritize and eliminate

Case Study of a Male • 77

those creative but not workable options, he lines through "win the lottery" to eliminate that option. His prioritized listing includes, "saving; and plan for the future."

The TC offers the **Reality-testing** prompt and Harry continues with his prioritized list, "saving → trim budget—watch spending; plan for future → already doing." His initial attention is to hone into to what he has identified as his main concern, and his responses are both reflections with additional thoughts to be considered.

Sustained Attention

The TC observed Harry's *sustained attention* as he continued with his investment in problem solving; he clearly **Identified** his **focus**, "How will I pay bills?" The **Encourage** prompt is designed to facilitate investment in creating possible change. The prompts orient the participant to examine the Steps to their *Best Plan* and the *Timeline* for completion of each step. Harry reports, (1) Complete monthly expenses spreadsheet—continue to follow → started already—maintain ongoing; and (2) Budget for new baby → Baby coming this summer (July/August). Harry closes with a positive self-statement, "Thank God for everything."

Engagement Style

Harry has not offered much new information; however, this presentation is much more focused, unlike the first problem-solving exchange that was reflective and passive. While Harry initially was not engaged, displaying a **Potential engagement style** with the first problem-solving session, this second time, Harry offers the same challenge as before. However, this time he creates a focal question that is within his control to develop a solution, then with that problem focus extended his investment with the development of a resolution plan. His solution again *does* go beyond what he has already been monitoring, he has a plan. At that point, Harry's engagement style is that of a **Goal-focused** engagement. Harry's focused attention is oriented to his resolution, demonstrating sustained attention. In completing a survey after the visit, Harry reports, "Once I identify a goal, no one can stop me in accomplishing what I set-out to accomplish."

FIRST YEAR FIRST SEMESTER: THIRD SESSION
PROCESSING TRANSITION

Initial Attention

Harry comes to visit with the TC and asks to problem-solve. She welcomes him and they visit briefly before she begins with a review of the ground rules. She offers the first prompt. "**Listen and List** challenges you are experiencing." Harry is familiar with the process, so he begins, "career change; classes— 'Busywork'; Test in April (Math 4–8 content)." Together they then move to the second prompt, "**Identify** your focus in a question form." Harry states, "What are the obstacles I am going through with my career change?"

78 • TEACHER CANDIDATE PROBLEM-SOLVING ENGAGEMENT STYLES

Harry then **Brainstorms**, "verbiage in classes; being a teacher; having my own classroom; making a good impression as a first-year teacher; how much support from mentors?" His brainstorming is reflective and when asked if he wants to eliminate any of his options, he says, "no." They then prioritize his recordings, which Harry indicates that he would like for each "to remain in the placement offered."

Reality Testing, Harry extends his brainstormed presentation, "(1) verbiage in classes → acronyms and general terms to educate; (2) being a teacher → stress; (3) having my own classroom → teamwork; (4) making a good impression as a first-year teacher → afraid of failure; (5) being a perfectionist → striving; (6) how much support form mentors?" → help with general questions."

Sustained attention

When asked to "**Identify** a focus in a question form," Harry states, "What are the obstacles I am going through with my career change?" This question is open-ended; however, it is more reflective. Harry is observed as being in this self-talk monolog rather than in an action-directed investment. This self-reflection continues as Harry progresses to the **Encourage** prompt (the limbs of LMSF) (1) Best Steps and Timelines are completed for each step. His response is, "(1) Research online—verbiage → now; (2) give it some time → ongoing; (3) Moodle → already utilizing Moodle; (4) research/ask question of teachers and observe model → ongoing—find a healthy teacher."

Engagement Style

Other than the one **Encourage** step with the "now" timeline, all of Harry's action steps are steps he has already assumed. This problem solving is also reflective rather than attentive in his investment. Harry appears guarded in his problem solving, and as such, again presents with a **Potential Engagement style**. One could assume that the person is not attentive or invested; however, given Harry's past academic success, and his multicultural background, one is left to assume that this is a problem-solving style preference. Harry concludes offering "self" a positive mantra, "You can do it."

FIRST YEAR FIRST SEMESTER: FOURTH SESSION

Initial Attention

The TC greets Harry as they discuss changes that have been occurring. Harry indicates he is ready to begin their problem solving, so they review ground rules, and the TC offers the first **Listen and List** prompt. Harry responds by listing what is on his mind, "exams; summer school; and new baby—August." They then con-

Case Study of a Male • 79

tinue with the second **Identify your focus** prompt. Harry's question is, "What are the pre-stressors/pressure of passing the exam?"

As they continue with the **Brainstorming** prompt, Harry states, "study more; have more resources; and have more review sessions provided by the program." When asked if he wants to eliminate any of the options, he says "no." His prioritized list remains the same, so they continue with the **Reality testing** prompt. Harry refers to his listing as he continues, "study more → hard with family—getting time; have more resources → online courses/tests and more study materials; and have more review sessions provided by the program → program increasing review time."

Sustained Attention

Harry's focal question, "What are the pre-stressors/pressure of passing the exam?" The TC reviews his reflections and then offers the **Encourage** prompt which contains the *Best Steps Plan* and *Timeline*. Harry's plan is to "study—spend & set aside more time → already started—keep going" is his timeline.

Engagement Style

Harry's preference to filter and internalize his attention without processing within the problem-solving setting continues. This approach suggests non-action attentiveness and reflective investment. He does not offer any displayed plans or timelines, and there is a lack of specificity to his process. This too, could suggest that Harry does not have a commitment to change, however, he is already doing what needs to be done to address his identified problem. He does not have a real problem to articulate or address. This session was identified as Harry holding a **Potential Engagement Style** preference.

FIRST YEAR SECOND SEMESTER: FIFTH SESSION

Initial Attention

Harry entered the session ready to engage. The TC welcomed him, reviewed the ground rules, and allowed him the space and time to process. She offered the first prompt, **Listen and List** challenges. Harry replied with, "three classes; death of uncle and grandmother haven't hit me yet; and balancing life—especially family." When asked the second prompt, **Identify a focal concern**, he replied: "How can I balance my personal life with school?" And his **Brainstorming** continued, "have more time for myself; go fishing; yard work; watching sports; and play PlayStation." He did not want to eliminate any of his options, and he indicated that he was pleased with the prioritized order he created so they moved forward to **Reality test**. Harry extended his brainstormed options with behavioral action investment: "(1) have more time for myself → sit back and set time aside; (2)

80 • TEACHER CANDIDATE PROBLEM-SOLVING ENGAGEMENT STYLES

go fishing →stay a day or a weekend; (3) yard work → improve year—anything that the wife wants; (4) watching sports → football, basketball, baseball <he then interrupted to add, difficult to find time>; and (5) play PlayStation → completing the goal, not do all that often."

Sustained Attention

The **Identified focus**, "How do I balance my personal life with school?" was holding all his attention as he moved into the final prompt, *Encourage* with *Steps to his Best solution* and *Timelines*. His plan included: "(1) yard work—easiest plant live oak trees, fix fence → immediately; (2) fishing → whenever brother-in-law calls and says let's go fishing; and (3) watching sports → immediately—Saturday." And his personal word of encouragement, "My Family."

Engagement Style

The TC comments included Harry's attentiveness to each prompt and willingness to attend. She indicated that there had been a re-scheduled visit because of Harry's uncle's death. They spoke of his uncle's death and the grieving process. Harry also mentioned that he and his wife were going to have a baby boy over the summer. During the problem solving, Harry selected to focus on balance and his sustained attention to that topic reflected that of a **Goal Focused Engagement Style**.

FIRST YEAR SECOND SEMESTER: SIXTH SESSION

Initial Attention

As with Harry's earlier problem-solving exchange, he came in with only one thought in mind, "group project." And his **focus** to that group project topic continued, "How can I continue group activities without a group?" He is now familiar with the prompts and process, so he is ready to **Brainstorm**, "take it at one step at a time; not do it; and go by professor's office." The TC invites Harry to delete any options that are not workable for him, he indicates that he would like to eliminate, "not do it." His priority listing is: (1) "take it at one step at a time" and he begins his **Reality Testing** by stating, "using check list and prioritizing," and continues, (2) "go by professor's office → talk about situation move."

Sustained Attention

Harry's focal concern is, "How can I continue group activities without a group?" His **Encourage** prompt detailed his *Steps to his Best Solution* and *Timelines*, which included, "(1) prioritize—most important to least and shift class time/study time → today; and (2) meet with professor during offices next week." Harry's word of encouragement, "My Family."

Engagement Style

The TC reports that Harry was always relaxed as he completed the prior LI-BRE Model problem-solving exchanges; however, this was not the case as he entered into the session this time. Harry reported that he had been experiencing stress regarding an upcoming group project and when he found out that the other group members had dropped the class leaving him alone with only one student who was currently being hospitalized, he decided to come in. He indicated that all was going well except for this one concern. His problem solving reflected this singular concern, "How can I continue group activities without a group?" The focus was to this concern and to the detailed resolution, which suggests that Harry was exhibiting a **Goal Focused Engagement Style**.

FIRST YEAR SECOND SEMESTER: SEVENTH SESSION

Initial Attention

Harry reported feeling frustrated. His tone reflected his resolved demeanor. He tells the TC what has gone on through the program. He explains that he has been told that there will be delays in pursuing his clinical teaching. He is not happy; however, on a positive note, he indicates that things are going well at home. After ground rules have been reviewed; then the TC offers the first prompt, **Listen and List**. Harry offers two concerns, "final project, and scheduling clinical teaching delay." When offered the **Identify focus** prompt, Harry reports, "What can I do about my clinical teaching being delayed?"

He then continues with **Brainstorming**, which includes: "meet with Dr. Bill again and stop coming to school." When asked if he wants to eliminate any of his options, he says, "yes, you can eliminate—stop coming to school." This left him with only one option to **Reality-test**. Harry explains, "Wait for response to email I sent."

Sustained Attention

Harry continues to focus on, "What can I do about my clinical teaching being delayed?" When the TC offered the **Encourage** prompt with the ***Best Steps*** and ***Timelines***, he reports, "(1) meet with Dr. Bill → when he is available and (2) the rest is out of my hands at this point." His mantra is "Getting through Program."

Engagement Style

Harry came into the session frustrated and he continued to vent, even as he repeated himself. He was not pleased with being informed of the delay and teetered between actions he had taken thus far and feelings of "the rest is out of my hands" therefore the TC assigned a **Venting Engagement Style** to this exchange.

PROBLEM-SOLVING PSYCHOSOCIAL
EXPRESSION FIRST YEAR SUMMARY

Harry entered the program with numerous reflective expressions. His initial engagement style was **Potential**, which is suggestive of persons that prefer to filter what they share and how they share information. This engagement style orients toward a passive, no action investment. Over this first year, Harry exhibited this **Potential Engagement Style** two additional times, and with each expression, the TC saw the engagement style as associated with school. Harry exhibited a **Venting Engagement Style** that similarly frames the problem in a non-action-oriented manner and offers a non-action-oriented resolution plan. Harry expressed this second, non-action-oriented engagement style, about a school concern. Venting usually occurs when an individual does not feel they have any control of what is occurring; thus, the response to vent. Harry appeared to move from Potential to Venting as he expressed his concerns with school. His reported identity in each of these cases was that of a student.

Harry implemented a **Goal Focused Engagement Style** two times with personal challenges. He also became **Goal Focused** once with a school concern. Of interest, is the gradient similarity of Potential to Goal focused; both engagement styles initially filter environmental contextual occurrences, Initial Attention. The difference occurs with the allocated Sustained Attention. With a goal focused engagement style, attention is action-oriented with the identification of the challenge; there is no notable attention to context other than to identify it. This was the case with Harry, and he used **goal focused** engagement styles to address school, financial (personal), and personal concerns. Each engagement style served a purpose for Harry. His narrative suggests that he is more comfortable filtering information by himself before investing externally. This also suggests that his potential engagement was reflective of how he managed himself.

SECOND YEAR FIRST SEMESTER: EIGHTH SESSION

The first year of course work has been completed. The expectation is that the second year will involve internship and field experiences in a school setting.

Initial Attention

Harry came into the session with a singularity of mind. After he and the TC exchanged greetings, he asked if they could begin. The TC agreed, reviewed the ground rules, and offered the first prompt, **Listen and List**. Harry offered, "generalist exam and job;" and moved on to the **Identify** a focus prompt, "How will I find a job?"

The TC then offered the **Brainstorm** prompt, which triggered a quick response, "look outside the districts; make me more marketable; substituting and consider

Case Study of a Male • 83

Palo Alto." Harry then responded that he was ready to **Reality test** and continued his listing as stated, "(1) look outside the districts → smaller outside districts, academics, other districts; (2) make myself more marketable → generalist exam, take this semester; (3) substituting → go to districts and sub for whatever is available, apply at districts for sub lists; and (4) consider Palo Alto → apply for positions in math."

Sustained Attention

Harry's **Identified concern** is clear, "How will I find a job?" As he begins the **Encourage** step, he carefully develops his ***Best Solution*** and ***Timeline***, "(1) update resume → already started—contacted career sites and Googled teacher resume templates, (2) Find out more about my certification contract, see Ms. Wise → already started, (3) apply at districts (outside) → already started, (4) start using my contacts → already started, and (5) generalist exam → sometime this semester." Harry closed with a mantra that addressed his focus, "My Family."

Engagement Style

Harry exhibited a **Goal focused Engagement Style** from the onset to the close of the session. He had one focus, which was sustained to the close—"How will I find a job?" Harry considered what factors are within his control, and ability to manage when he framed his goal. He also developed a solution that would create change.

SECOND YEAR FIRST SEMESTER: NINTH SESSION

Initial Attention

Harry enters the room with a flat expression. "How will I find a job when the program continues changing things?" The TC asks Harry if he is ready to begin his problem solving and he says "yes." She reviews the ground rules and then offers the first prompt, **Listen and List** challenges you are experiencing; Harry's response, "trying to find a job and program changes." As they move to the second focal concern, Harry re-states, "How will I find a job when the program continues changing things?" They then begin to **Brainstorm**; however, Harry only has one response, "program meeting is coming up." Then extending his thinking to the **Reality testing**, Harry continues, "attend on Friday for information." Simple single responses: nothing more is offered.

Sustained Attention

The TC follows Harry's pace, and they review his work and the **Identified concern**, "How will I find a job when the program continues changing things?"

84 • TEACHER CANDIDATE PROBLEM-SOLVING ENGAGEMENT STYLES

As Harry began the **Encourage** step with the **Best Steps** and **Timelines**, his only response was to repeat what he had already offered, "Attend the program meeting. I can't do anything else until I find out what the program people say → Friday at 5:30."

Engagement Style

Harry has returned to a **Potential engagement style.** This filtered non-action and limited investment, operates as a processing place for Harry. While he may be feeling helpless, he does not vent, rather he filters his communication to one of limited observable investment and attention.

SECOND YEAR FIRST SEMESTER: TENTH SESSION

Initial Attention

Harry entered the session with a smile. He reported that his clinical teaching was going well. He also indicated that he was obtaining experience and enjoying working with the students. The TC and Harry talked about his future goals and he indicated he was planning on becoming an administrator. In reference to family, Harry said that they were processing a daycare situation with his youngest child and the family was adjusting well to his clinical teaching schedule changes. The TC asked if he was ready to problem-solve and he said, "yes." They began with a review of the ground rules and moved into the first prompt, **Listen and List**; Harry listed only one item, "Portfolio (due this semester)." The TC then offered the second **Identify a Focal Concern**, Harry offered, "What do I need to do to complete my portfolio?"

Harry's familiarity with the process made him feel at ease as he **Brainstormed**, "attend Portfolio session; and build on what I have from other classes." When asked if he wanted to eliminate any of his options, his response was immediate, "no." He then prioritized the listed options and he said he wanted to use the listing as presented. They then moved to the **Reality Testing**. Harry extended his original list adding the response to the reality testing: "(1) attend Portfolio session → Monday at 5:30 (Main campus) and receive a better understanding of requirements; and (2) build on what I have from other classes → Dr. Pete's class materials."

Sustained Attention

Harry was ready to continue with his **Identified Concern**, "What do I need to do to complete my portfolio?" so they move to the **Encourage** prompt with **Best Step Solutions** and **Timelines**. His engagement is detailed as he reports, "(1) attend portfolio session on main campus → Monday at 5:30; (2) Implement information I receive there → after Monday's meeting; and (3) gather what I have

Case Study of a Male • 85

started from my other courses and build on it → next week and continue over semester." No other information is provided, and no positive word is offered.

Engagement Style

Harry entered the session with an action-oriented stance, and while he did not offer much detail to his current life worldview, he was immediate in identifying what he wanted to problem-solve. Once he stated his focal concern, he remained attentive to the next steps that facilitated the change he wanted to manage. With this session, the TC observed Harry as maintaining a **Goal focused Engagement Style.**

SECOND YEAR SECOND SEMESTER: ELEVENTH SESSION

Initial Attention

Harry's presentation of self was consistent with his earlier visits. He expressed he was feeling tired, which he attributed to his schedule. He also mentioned that his son had been sick this week. He shared that the first observation report he received was positive and mentioned that he had turned in his portfolio and he felt good about the accomplishment. After their initial check-in, the TC asked if Harry was ready to begin. His response was, "yes." She offered the review of the ground rules and offered the first **Listen and List** prompt; Harry's response, "lesson plans; learning how to incorporate 2 grade levels behind as well." He re-stated his **Identified Focal Concern** as, "How can I prepare for teaching days/ lesson plans?" before moving to the **Brainstorming** which included: "(1) talk to Mary and ask her to look at my plans; (2) print out schedule from last year's plan; and (3) classroom management." He then explains that his listing was prioritized and that he did not want to eliminate any of his options. They continued as the TC offered the Reality testing prompt; as before, he extended his behavioral action by asking that an arrow be extended to his *"What it would look like responses?"* They included, "(1) talk to Mary and ask her to look at my plans → bring up questions— next week; (2) print out schedule from last year's plan → not helpful since not the same; and (3) classroom management → discuss with content teacher and bring myself to their level with the vocabulary and understanding." The TC reviewed his reflections and asked if he was ready to develop his plan.

Sustained Attention

Harry said, "yes," as he looked at his **Identified Focused Question**, "How can I prepare for teaching days/lesson plans?" They quickly moved into the **Encourage *Steps to the Best Solution*** and ***Timeline*** space. Harry's plan, "(1) use technology → already doing it—continue; (2) ask Maria my questions → next week; and (3) talk with my content teacher → Monday." When asked if he had a word of

86 • TEACHER CANDIDATE PROBLEM-SOLVING ENGAGEMENT STYLES

encouragement to offer himself, he said, "nope." They closed and Harry said he would let her know how this went.

Engagement Style

Harry's **Goal-focused Engagement Style** work was straightforward and modified as he moved across the LIBRE Model prompts; by the time he completed the problem solving, he had created a plan with timelines for managing his next steps.

SECOND YEAR SECOND SEMESTER: TWELFTH SESSION

This is Harry's final problem-solving exchange. He came in agitated and frustrated with the clinical class.

Initial Attention

The TC greeted Harry and noting that he was upset, she asked if she could assist. He nodded "yes" that he wanted to problem-solve. She reviewed the ground rules before offering the first **Listen and List** prompt. His responses were, "family, house in Seguin, creating lesson plans, content teacher planning the lessons, content teacher not using lesson plans," and closed his listing by saying that the "content teacher has major control issues." The TC then asked him to **Identify a focal concern**, to which Harry stated, "Why am I creating lesson plans and my content teacher is not allowing me to use them?"

They then moved to the **Brainstorming** and **Reality-testing** prompts. The TC observed Harry as becoming repetitious. The TC recorded the responses and noted that he was talking to himself as he repeated his thoughts. His ruminations were as follows: "stop doing lesson plan; ask content teacher to let me use my lesson plan so I can learn; continue to create lesson plans; and stop going to school." When asked if there were any options he wanted to eliminate, he said "Yes. Stop doing the lesson plans and stop going to school; the others are okay." His reality testing was a repeat, "actually create lesson plans and continue to create lesson plans." The TC reviewed Harry's work with him before moving to the Encourage prompt.

Sustained Attention

Harry listened but remained in his own self-reflect space, "Why am I creating lesson-plans and my content teacher is not allowing me to use them?" As they moved to the final **Encourage** prompt *Best Steps* and *Timelines*, Harry said, "(1) continue to create lesson plans → I have to start this week because I only have a limited amount of time; (2) spend extra time on creating lesson plans." He said thanks for the time and said he needed to leave. The session closed and the TC did not offer any additional words of encouragement.

TABLE 7.1.   Harry's Problem Solving Data Narrative

Problem-Solving Session	Identity/Context	Problem Solving Approach	Challenge Focus
First Session: Interview for the Program	Unemployed/Job	Potential Engagement Style	Taking time off from work – financially
Second Session: Spring First Semester	Unemployed/Job	Goal-Focused Engagement Style	How will I pay bills?/ Within his control
Third Session: Spring First Semester	Career/Job	Potential Engagement Style	What are the obstacles I am going through with my career change?/ Within his control
Fourth Session: Spring First Semester	Student/School	Potential Engagement Style	What are the pre-stresses/pressure of passing the exam?/Within his control
Fifth Session: Fall Second Semester	Student/School	Goal-focused Engagement Style	How can I balance my personal life w/school?/ Within his control
Sixth Session: Fall Second Semester	Student/School	Goal-focused Engagement Style	How can I continue group activities without a group?/Within his control
Seventh Session: Fall Second Semester	Student/School	Venting Engagement Style	What can I do about my clinical teaching being delayed?/Outside his control
Eighth Session: Fall Second Semester	Student & Career/School & Job	Goal-focused Engagement Style	How will I find a job?/ Within his control
Ninth Session: Spring Third Semester	Student & Career/School & Job	Potential Engagement Style	How can I find a job when the program keeps changing things?/Outside his control
Tenth Session: Spring Third Semester	Student/School	Goal-focused Engagement Style	What do I need to do to complete my portfolio?/ Within his control
Eleventh Session: Fall Fourth Semester	Student/School	Goal-focused Engagement Style	How can I prepare for my teaching days/lesson plans? /Within his control
Twelfth Session: Fall Fourth Semester	Student/School	Venting Engagement Style	Why am I creating lesson plans and my content teacher is not allowing me to use them?

Engagement Style

This was a difficult moment for Harry; however, he used the safety of the problem-solving session to vent—thus, the **Venting Engagement Style.** There was more emotional self-talk exchanged in response to the now familiar prompts. No real action, no real goal and a sense of needing to keep doing what he has been doing—as stated with the repetition.

PROBLEM-SOLVING PSYCHOSOCIAL EXPRESSION SECOND YEAR SUMMARY

This second year, Harry was observed implementing a great span of emotion as he processed the transition from class to field experiences and internship. The TC also observed shifts in engagement styles to better meet his needs. For example, he vented with the TC to not jeopardize his professional presentation in the class and/or in the school settings. The problem-solving sessions with the TC became a safe place to move away from the filtered potential engagement style to vent. This second year he became much more goal-focused in how he managed change. The time with the TC and familiarity with the LIBRE Model assisted him in his newly developing teacher role. The TC became a relationally supportive resource that allowed him to be resilient across the numerous identity roles, (as a student, and as a student teacher) and context (in the classroom, in the school); allowing him to present himself well.

ENGAGEMENT STYLE SUMMARY

Harry experienced many changes and challenges, not only at school, but also with his family. Two members of his family died over this period and a new baby was born; the largest changes occurred as he went from being a civil engineer, to a banker, to becoming a math teacher. By the close of this experience, a predominant Goal Focused Engagement Style best met his personal and professional processing needs. He was observed in this engagement style six times over the course of the two years. While he initially began the program with a Potential Engagement Style, the TC observed him maintaining the filtered Initial Attention, but shifted to action and the Goal Focused management of his identified challenges. This profile suggests that Harry is most comfortable observing and reflecting rather than initiating actions. Only two times did he vent about school changes; however, he was attentive to share that information only with the TC in a setting in which he would not be perceived in a negative light. With these two action-investments, he did not sustain an action-orientation, he actively initially engaged only to pull-back and close the session in his preferred reflective investment mode.

In conversation with the TC, she indicated that Harry graduated and was hired in the school where he had completed his internship. He was, and continues to be successful as a math teacher, and he was reported to have left to teach in a second district that offered him an increased salary.

SECTION 3

ENGAGEMENT STYLE IMPLICATIONS ON SELF-MANAGEMENT AND DEVELOPMENT

CHAPTER 8

ECOLOGICAL MULTICULTURAL MODEL

This chapter focuses on engagement styles by exploring identity and context with the APA multicultural model lens (APA, 2017). To accomplish this review, we revisit the two teacher candidates. We begin with their identified roles as entry graduate full-time students. They are members of an education cohort that provides a transitional coach to facilitate the anticipated changes that occur with an accelerated teacher education program. Each teacher candidate is provided a series of problem-solving exchanges. A transitional coach used the LIBRE Model (Guerra, 2009, 2015, 2016) to collect the data, which includes roles, context, identified problems, and selected resolution plans. The teacher candidates learn to be aware of their allocation of attention and preferred engagement styles. They receive feedback and learn to manage their attentiveness to their varied contexts (e.g., school, home, work).

Chapter 6 examined the female problem-solver, Sharon; Chapter 7 examined the male problem-solver, Harry. It was not the intent to represent all persons in problem-solving roles; rather, the goal is to identify different individual expressions of attention, identified roles, and contexts and how these factors intersect as each student pursued an education degree and teaching certificate. There is an unaddressed notion that students enter classrooms ready to learn without outside

---

Teacher Candidate Problem-Solving Engagement Styles:
LIBRE Model Self-Management Analysis, pages 91–97.
Copyright © 2022 by Information Age Publishing
www.infoagepub.com
All rights of reproduction in any form reserved.

life interference. The gap between study and practice is the larger question we explore; how do graduate students' problem-solve, engage in the classroom, and outside? When we consider support, culture, role, and context, do these relate to their selected engagement styles?

This revisit examines the expressed multiple identities and intersectionality of each teacher candidate. The LIBRE Model facilitator serves as an external relational support for teacher candidates transitioning across multiple identities. Engagement styles are self-reported within their identities, in addition to their perceived understandings of identified contexts and investments. This APA review considers culture and context in relation to the teacher candidates selected outcomes. This examination facilitates how teacher candidates view their multiple contexts, cultures, investment, engagements and outcome; all which support their acknowledged roles.

To illustrate, we begin this discussion with the female student. Sharon reported multiple identities/roles: mother, wife, daughter, employee, and student. At times these roles collided. She selected the APA Level 4. self-management fluid forward path to address the larger social context addressed at the APA Level 5., the larger level outcome. She was determined to accommodate external needs to meet her professional development and career path needs.

FEMALE TEACHER CANDIDATE

APA Guideline 1. Importance of Identity and Self-definition as fluid and complex. Sharon expresses three distinct identities: (1) employee/worker at the university; (2) family identity that includes daughter, wife, and mother; and (3) student at the university, a teacher candidate of an accelerated teacher preparation program.

APA Guideline 2. Cultural attitudes and beliefs influence perception. Sharon expresses three distinct cultural attitudes and beliefs that influence her perception. Belonging to a traditional conservative Latino family is fundamental to her identity. Sharon was raised within a context whose values, mores, and tenets shape and influence her worldview. She has strong ties to her parents who live close to her. She is also married and carries those traditions and family values to her family, as a wife and mother.

Sharon's second cultural and contextual beliefs are associated with being an employee at the university. While this identity and context is mentioned as a lesser-valued belief, it is a part of her until graduating from the university with her master's degree to assume a teacher role, which will eventually offer her a promotion to a higher paid position. Sharon's third cultural context is that of student and teacher candidate within a master's degree program within a university setting.

APA Guideline 3. Language and Communication are expressed through engagement. Sharon's engagement styles and variations suggest that there were considerations which influenced how and what she attended to. For example, as a mother, she focuses all of her attention (actual engagement) on her son's challenges with reading; however, as she attends to Christmas, she shifts to a more direct goal-focused engagement. Finally, Sharon exhibits a potential engagement style as she considers her son's entry into middle school. While all are linked to the same family identity, her engagement, the way she processed and assumed distinct roles differed, depending on the identified challenge and how she framed it. Sharon's second acknowledged identity was that of a university employee; however, Sharon never attended her employment as a focal investment. Rather, she indicates it as a contextual factor to consider as she problem-solves spending more time with her husband. Sharon reported that her employment and corresponding identity as an employee are well managed.

Sharon's third role and identity proved to be a dominating feature. She stated her identity as student in a higher education context. Of the ten problem-solving exchanges, six involved the university context in which Sharon assumed the role as teacher candidate. Of those six events, Sharon consistently responds with an actual engagement style that is characterized as holding a consistent attention from the beginning to the end of the social exchange. Only one school problem-solving event impacted her differently. Sharon was challenged in preparing her lesson plans ahead of time. Her responsibility was to make the necessary adaptations for the special-needs child using the regular class lesson plans. She expressed this challenge as, "teachers have not been creating their lesson plans ahead of time → so I cannot modify my plans ahead of time." Here, Sharon assumed a venting engagement style within this role and context.

APA Guideline 4. Social and physical context influence views of environment. Sharon was adaptive to her various social and physical contexts; she was aware of her environments and adjusted herself to accommodate her identities. The LIBRE Model facilitator played an important role with Sharon's transitions and intersections. She becomes a sounding board and recorder of patterns from which Sharon can move and negotiate. At some points, Sharon makes family her single focus; for example, with Christmas approaching, Sharon moves all her focus to respond to the concern, "How do I have the Christmas presents under the tree by the 24th?"

APA Guideline 5. Historical and contemporary experiences with power, privilege, and oppression. The facilitator supports Sharon's views of power, privilege, and oppression to operationalize each exchange as an event in which Sharon does have some control (even if it is only of herself). She also provided Sharon relational support to seek resolution, which was helpful, particularly when Sharon did not have any power or privilege with the context (as student teacher), and when she is experiencing (what she perceived as system) oppression when the teachers she was to work with did not complete their work. We see this in those times that she vents about how she is not able to complete her lesson plans ahead of time because those in position and power are not completing their assigned work. While not a historic oppression, the situational oppression does provide a challenge and if Sharon would have had prior negative oppressive events, this "private venting with the TC" could have been expressed in a less diplomatic forum.

94 • TEACHER CANDIDATE PROBLEM-SOLVING ENGAGEMENT STYLES

APA Guideline 6. Culturally adaptive interventions and advocacy. Strength-based problem solving becomes a culturally adaptive intervention that helps advocacy. The facilitator, in relationship with Sharon, allowed Sharon to express herself unfiltered in a safe space. It is here that she had time to think, write, and reflect. Together they examined and re-examined Sharon's plans before she assumed any action. This allowed Sharon the freedom to practice new roles with new contexts under a low stake setting, so that when she actually moved into that new role, she had already practiced and honed her skills. This "side bar processing with the TC" provided Sharon with some leadership consultation and development so, rather than react, she is able to identify needs and advocate for a resolution.

APA Guideline 7. The profession's self-examination of assumptions and practices within a global context and the impact upon self-definition, purpose, role and function. The TC works within a community of other TC counselors. They collaborate and work under a supervisor trained in mental health services, and in full disclosure, is the developer of the LIBRE Model (Guerra, 2009). Each time Sharon met with the TC, there was time to re-connect and examine past problem-solving exchanges, what worked, what did not work and what/if the challenge remained. Their revisits, then, would lead to discussions of personal assumption to global context.

APA Guideline 8. Developmental stages and life transitions intersect with larger biosociocultural context to influence worldviews and identity. Sharon continues to favor her actual engagement style over time and context; this became a biosociocultural context for her. By the last session, she is recognized for her skill and management as she processes her own question, "How to prepare to present my point of view to the principal and other teacher?" She approaches this topic with an actual engagement style, self-confident as a resilient professional. Interestingly, Sharon does not have that same confidence as a mom, and asks, "How can I adjust to my son being in middle school?" The developmental stage of one person brings context and complexity to others. In this case, Sharon's son's transition to middle school impacts Sharon and her own adjustment to this developmental stage in her family unit.

APA Guideline 9. Culturally appropriate and informed research, teaching, supervision, consultation and evaluation of efficacy. Over this two-year period, the transitional coach monitors Sharon's responses and facilitated these processes so she was able to benefit from the culturally appropriate and informed research, even as she receives supervision and consultation. Self-efficacy and student supported success are their underlying goals. She learned the culture of the school, of her new role, even as she reexamined her family roles.

APA Guideline 10. Educators, like psychologists, are mindful to seek strength-based approaches that build resilience within sociocultural contexts. The problem-solving approach fostered growth and development. It provided an open space for participants to consider their contexts and express their challenges, with

Ecological Multicultural Model • 95

the freedom to focus on one issue at a time. Similarly, as a strength-based approach, if participants choose not to complete the problem-solving activity, the transitional coach still offers encouragement to motivate them at any level of involvement without any judgement.

The goal is to support the teacher candidates and teach the self-regulated skills so they can enter the workforce prepared to meet complex challenges. As researchers, we are aware that the need for highly skilled teachers is great, and recognize the "context of the larger need," the self-awareness to manage diverse needs of their students within a changing teaching profession. There needs to be provision for self-reflection. Without the security and self-reflection change will not occur. This intervention embraced in the learned patterns of engagement and introduced context and observed patterns to assist the teacher candidates in developing strategic, agile engagement styles to maximize their professional success.

Let us now revisit the male teacher candidate. He entered the program with a distinct engagement style, that of potential with limited initial and sustained attention. The multiple roles and contextual challenges he encountered were met provided him with a different recorded resilience path

MALE TEACHER CANDIDATE

APA Guideline 1. Importance of Identity and Self-definition as fluid and complex. Harry expresses two distinct identities: (1) a family identity that includes son, husband, and father, and (2) a graduate student at the university identity, and a teacher candidate of an accelerated teacher preparation program. Harry mentions that his father is Latino, and his mother is White.

APA Guideline 2. Cultural attitudes and beliefs influence perception. Individuals are raised within contexts that include values, mores, and tenets. The multiple cultures shape and influence their worldviews. Harry grew-up in two different cultural worlds, that of his mother and that of his father. He laments spending more time with his mother's White culture than with his father's Latino culture. The way Harry presented his engagement transitions with problem solving suggests he is aware and interacts in different ways as he transitions from one culture to another culture. Harry shares his attitudes and beliefs, which in turn influence his perception. He was definitive in what he was willing to process and what he considered as off-limits.

APA Guideline 3. Language and Communication are expressed through engagement. Harry's background across cultures was seen in his preferred engagement style identified as potential, given his filtered and non-committal language. Harry restates previous actions in his initial problem-solving exchange, which means he was not proposing any actions beyond what he is already doing. At one point, he mentions that he likes to be out in the country where he can walk and think freely. He values communication with self.

APA Guideline 4. Social and physical context influence views of environment. The transitional coach is supportive of Harry in his transitions across various school and personal contexts. His initial attention continues to be filtered, however, there are incremental changes in his sustained attention as he becomes goal-focused to address both the personal and student concerns. Socially, he presents himself as a private person who does not favor direct contextual influence.

APA Guideline 5. Historical and contemporary experiences with power, privilege, and oppression. Harry is deliberate in his problem solving and communication investment; he is sensitive to power and privilege and vents on two occasions about the school system changes and the limited power that he, as a student has, "Why am I creating lesson plans and my content teacher is not allowing me to use them?"

APA Guideline 6. Culturally adaptive interventions and advocacy. Strength-based problem solving becomes a culturally adaptive intervention that facilitates advocacy. The transitional coach role allows Harry to express himself with his filtered preference and without judgment in a safe space. Harry is able to take time to think, write, and reflect. He is given an opportunity to develop plans that can then be re-examined before any actions are taken. This allows Harry the freedom to practice the new teacher role with new contexts under low stakes settings so that when he actually moves into that new role, he has experienced some practice and honing of skills.

APA Guideline 7. The profession's self-examination of assumptions and practices within a global context and the impact upon self-definition, purpose, role and function. The transitional coach works within a community of other transitional counselors. They collaborate and work under a supervisor who is also trained in mental health services. Harry and the transitional coach visit to re-examine his engagement styles, context, and roles to give him a better context of his larger school and work context.

APA Guideline 8. Developmental stages and life transitions intersect with larger biosociocultural context to influence worldviews and identity. Harry continues to favor his potential engagement style; he enjoys the processing over time and contextual factors are examined as he contemplates outside the problem-solving exchanges. Harry's pattern of engagement is predominately potential, a processing investment; he did however, select a goal-focused engagement on one occasion. By the last session, he is recognized for his strength-based skills and management as he processes the self-identified question, "Why am I creating lesson plans and my content teacher is not allowing me to use them?" He approaches this with a venting engagement style and with the self-confidence of a resilient professional.

APA Guideline 9. Culturally appropriate and informed research, teaching, supervision, consultation and evaluation of efficacy. Harry received a culturally appropriate and informed intervention/problem-solving exchange. After the TC researched persons from multicultural backgrounds, she was able to better understand the processing of challenges Harry was experiencing, and she was able to support him, even though they never overtly discussed culture. Self-efficacy and student supported success were Harry's underlying goals; for Harry, these filtered communications allowed him the freedom to process as he selected to process.

APA Guideline 10. Educators like psychologist should seek Strength-based approaches to build resilience within sociocultural contexts. This strength-based problem-solving approach is designed and used to meet an identified professional need. This need is not only for highly skilled teachers, but for the larger context; a professional need that will likely not change without intervention. The intervention, which may entail learning skills of self-awareness monitoring, self-management in developing and monitoring plans and/or self-regulation, is designed to become balanced, skilled, culturally efficacious teachers; teachers who value self and have a value of others.

SUMMARY

Both teacher candidates expressed different challenges. Each also assumed different identities in managing their stated concerns. Each had stylistic engagement preferences. Noted were the relationship between identity and engagement, which then contributed to their corresponding outcomes. The multicultural experience is complex and is best appreciated when examined through a multifaceted lens. The multifaceted lens makes it possible to see and appreciate the complexity of the multicultural experience.

REFERENCES

American Psychological Association. (2017). *Multicultural guidelines: An ecological approach to context, identity, and intersectionality.* http://www.apa.org/about/policy/multicultural-guidelines.pdf

Guerra, N. S. (2009). LIBRE stick figure tool: Graphic organizer. *Interventions in Schools and Clinics, 44*(4), 1–5.

Guerra, N. S. (2015). *Clinical problem-solving case management.* Rowman & Littlefield and Lexington Books.

Guerra, N. S. (2016). *Addressing challenges Latinos/as encounter with the LIBRE model: Listen-identify-brainstorm-reality-test-encourage.* Peter Lang Publishing.

CHAPTER 9

COMMUNITY-OF-SELF FROM AN ACTION RESEARCH LENS

This chapter provides a third revisit to the teacher candidates' problem-solving. This time the focus is directed toward the internal problem-solving dialogs each person had with the self, as they processed their LIBRE Model exchanges (Guerra, 2001, 2006). Vygotsky (1978) explained that individuals transform themselves through "labor and tool" use. These teacher candidates exhibited his described internal language (tools) use in processing identified challenges (labor). While we examined the teacher candidates' narratives individually in Chapters 6 and 7, this revisit looks at the teacher candidates as a group-of-self or *individuals-in-community.*

For example, Harry has a group dialog to address the same problem on two separate consecutive occasions; however, with two different approaches. In the first problem-solver (PS) exchange, he explains that his return to school will mean that his family will have limited resources; however, he has already made provisions for the shortfall. He assumed a reflective non-action-oriented approach to his problem. The second PS exchange had the exact same identified problem, but this time, his approach to the problem was with a focused investment on the development of an action-oriented resolution. Since these case studies are examined as group—expressions of self, a different investigative approach was selected.

Teacher Candidate Problem-Solving Engagement Styles:
LIBRE Model Self-Management Analysis, pages 99–105.
Copyright © 2022 by Information Age Publishing
www.infoagepub.com
All rights of reproduction in any form reserved.

99

100 • TEACHER CANDIDATE PROBLEM-SOLVING ENGAGEMENT STYLES

Methodologically, action research provides the ideal structure to explain this concept. Action research is designed to address a systematic study of *individuals in community* with the goal of identifying solutions to daily-confronted challenges (Stringer, 2007). Conversely, rather than individuals within a group, this review will adapt to include the notion of individual-as-a-group or *community-of-self.* *Community-of-self* is defined as the presentation of multiple roles, identities (culture, values), and context, in reciprocal interaction one-with-the-other to generate a personalized *engagement profile.* The *self-community* is the constant element, and referring to the above example, Harry not only continues his internal dialog with the same problem, he reflects additional language and thought, as he shifts his language and motivational approach. The community is represented in the multiple (two-year collection of LIBRE Model data points) problem-solving exchange and use of "language and tools."

ACTION RESEARCH ROUTINE

Stringer (2014) explains this "action research routine" as a series of continuing revisits to allow the participants a moment to step back and examine, rethink, reanalyze, and perhaps create change. This **Look-Think-Act** cycle allows for revisits to prior thoughts, reflection, and the reality-testing needed to assist with the development of change. Similarly, each teacher candidate **Looked** at the products created as observations were reviewed. The graphic organizer, the LMSF tool, facilitated this process. The PS's exact language and thoughts were recorded; thereby assisting their self-appraisal. The **Think** occurred as reflections and reanalysis occurred. From one problem-solving exchange to the next, the teacher candidate reviewed their prior work. The transitional coach problem-solving sessions included introductory check-ins to explore thoughts and/or actions that may have occurred since their last visit. The **Act** occurred as action, re-examine, and modification of outlined resolution plans occurred. The teacher candidates reflected with the TC, to revisit and evaluate their problem-solving and the effectiveness of their resolution plans and efforts.

ACTION RESEARCH APPLIED TO PROBLEM-SOLVING

We implemented the LIBRE Model Listening prompts to process the (open-ended) problem-solving events. As explained in prior chapters, environmental worldview of self, roles, and how best to manage conflict exchanges occurred, a myriad of changes occurred in each of these teacher candidates' lives, from the first LIBRE Model exchange in which a personal-constructed identity to the last exchange as graduates and teachers. The recorded participant data were then analyzed and shared with each additional exchange. The action research **Look-Think-Act** cycle fits well and provides the processing of background to the larger personal and professional development. Given the transformational changes that

Community-of-Self from an Action Research Lens • 101

the teacher candidates experience, the approach brings attention to the complexity of each as a member of a changing self-group.

PROBLEM-SOLVING HUMAN DEVELOPMENT

The LIBRE Model problem-solving exchanges showcase Bandura's social cognitive, Bronfenbrenner's social-ecological, and goal orientation constructs in the teacher candidate provided PS data. Bandura (2006) explains that each person represents a human agency, holding an active participation of his/her own life. The PS assumes this active role, often beginning the LIBRE Model exchange with family concerns resulting from returning to school. Bronfenbrenner's social-ecological model (1986) highlights the cultural value that individuals represent as situated members within a (family) system. Similarly, the PS presents context and values as challenges are introduced. For example, PS's spouses and/or friends, who also experience the social changes as they have occurred. The problem-solvers' brainstorming and reality-testing close the loop to what is identified as *Initial Attention*. The L-listen, B-brainstorming and R-reality testing provides information to the teacher candidates' environment, person, and behavior. Subsequent *Sustained Attention*, which includes identification of the problem, and the development of the solution with timelines are recorded. The problem-solving language provides the problem-solver points of distinctions that can then be addressed.

For example, as the participants are asked to identify a concern, this prompt motivationally invites attention toward action, with the description of context to the identified problem. At a closer look, the problem, is an investment in the individual and what that person believes is a singular goal. Schunk (2012) and Zimmerman (2000) address the importance of goal orientation in establishing a directional commitment to change. As defined in learning theory (Schunk, 1990), a performance goal is represented in one's focused attention to the identified task and perseverance to invest up to its completion (Schunk, 1990). The two case study presentations highlight the engagement features associated with self-reported (identity roles) human development, and challenges (problem-solving).

The three problem-solving questions explored were: (1) "What was the social context of concern (e.g., personal, work, school)?," (2) "What was the identity assumed in addressing the problem?" and (3) "What were the participants' *Initial* and *Sustained Attention* as they examined their problem, holistically representing their engagement style picture (Guerra, 2009)?"

COMMUNITY-OF-SELF CASES

Sharon was self-reflective in her engagement. Seven of the ten problem-solving exchanges were actual engagement investments; the detailed language of the initial attention to sustained attention highlighted her commitment to each identified context. For example, she assumed an actual engagement to process two family

102 • TEACHER CANDIDATE PROBLEM-SOLVING ENGAGEMENT STYLES

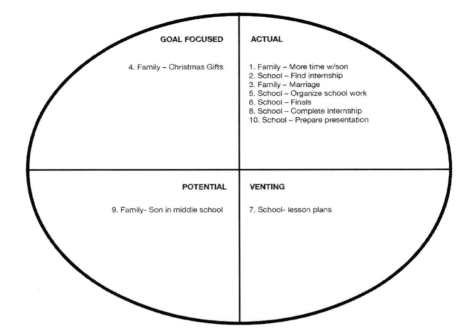

FIGURE 9.1 Sharon's Engagement Community-of-Self-Group

concerns—son and marriage; her self-reported role was mother and wife. The remaining five exchanges addressed school and her role as a student. Within this context, she implemented the same engagement style to process challenges with finding an internship, organizing her schoolwork, finals, completing her internship and preparing for a professional presentation. The only deviation from her actual engagement, over the two year period with three exchanges each year occurred: (1) when she assumed to a goal-focused engagement to address how she was going to get the family's presents under the Christmas tree; (2) when she assumed a venting engagement as she wondered how she could write up her lesson plans when the general education teachers were not developing their lesson plans—how could she make the necessary adjustments to their plans if their plans were not written?; and (3) deviation occurred when she reflected on her son going into middle school; her only expressed engagement was that of potential, (See Figure 9.1).

Harry was also self-reflective in his engagement with a different PS profile and approach. He began his problem-solving exchanges with a potential engagement; his language was guarded and reflective from initial attention to the closing sustained attention. His preferred potential engagement was observed with financial concerns, given his unemployment. He exhibited this same potential engaged

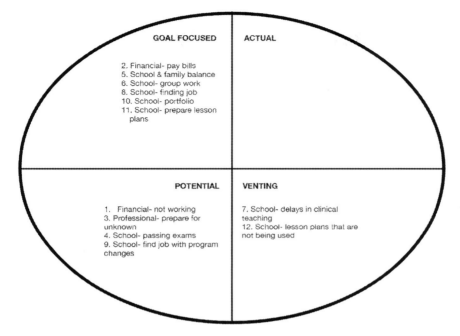

FIGURE 9.2. Harry's Community-of-Self Engagement

reflection as he considered the implications of preparing for an unknown profession and as he processed two school concerns: passing his exams and finding a job during program changes. His most observed dominant engagement style was that of a goal-focused engagement, which was observed while addressing school-related concerns. There were six exchanges that addressed this approach and all, but one, had school as the context. His primary role was that of student; he processed challenges that included paying bills, balancing school, and family, organizing schoolwork, completing his portfolio, and preparing lesson plans. He only deviated from his goal-focused engagement twice as he vented about delays in his clinical teaching and having to write lesson plans that were not being used.

Each candidate came to solutions that facilitated their sustaining success as teachers; each were processed differently. Sharon maintained an actual engagement with a defined actual engagement pattern, while Harry never approached actual engagement in his management of daily challenges. Harry's problem-solving was observed as having a filtered investment from the LIBRE Model, an initial attention to the sustained attention; he filtered the management of his defined contexts. His only goal-focused engagement was demonstrated as a sustained investment toward action and toward resolution when he was unable to resolve the challenge after addressing it using a potential engagement. Harry's engagements

104 • TEACHER CANDIDATE PROBLEM-SOLVING ENGAGEMENT STYLES

favored limited initial and sustained attention; however, a focal change in initial and invested sustained attention was observed as he moved from invested initial attention without sustained investment as he vented about school delays in clinical teaching and unused lesson plans.

While Harry too, had a distinct engagement style preference, each teacher candidate learned how to be self-aware and self-regulate their roles within each defined context and their selected engagement was observed in their outcome resolutions and follow-up reporting. They each found sustaining solutions in the self-regulated and managed response to change and challenge.

Closing Story. There are whole person needs that assist the development of wellbeing. Each student entered the teaching profession to serve the students found in our assigned schools. These college students were provided the opportunity to attend to their cultural roles and identities at home along with the new emerging identities associated with their higher education experiences. They were supported to learn self-awareness and how to self-regulate their engagement styles. Problem-solving and self-reflecting in a safe space are the experiences that the teacher candidates used to become self-regulated. Their self-reflection skills facilitated self-management as a wellness experience that was shared with others who were associated with these students. For the teacher candidates graduating from this contextual experience, they became master problem-solvers; well-fed intellectually, social-cognitively, and culturally. They graduated with years of health holistic learning and self-development application. Attentiveness to self and the allocation of attention was the first step to the examination of multiple identity roles experienced, even as they experienced and attempted to better understand the changes that they were personally experiencing, and decisions made.

CONCLUDING THOUGHTS

The action research framework was useful in describing the teacher candidate's personal and professional development. The teacher candidates regularly problem solve; their challenges were associated with their studies, contexts, and life changes. The action research "revisiting system" was helpful to their processing of personal changes which facilitated their professional development. For these two teacher candidates, the multiple problem-solving events displayed contexts, identities, roles, and engagement styles to create a larger interpersonal picture. Potential challenges, contexts, roles, and identities assumed become visible as problem-solving engagement patterns. The cumulative series of LIBRE Model problem-solving (analogous to community) were used to review experiences, to reflect, and re-visit the identified challenges. The scripted problem-solving exchanges parallel the shared space to process and represent the community. The action research routine facilitates the understanding of these identified pattern of events.

Each problem-solving exchange used the same five prompts to anchor the dialog and facilitate self-expressions, context, roles, and resolutions. Engagement styles were assessed with each exchange. As addressed with Sharon, who consistently preferred to be actively engaged; however, also noted was the major shift when her attention was directed to her role of mom, which resulted in her engagement style change to goal-focused. "How am I going to get Christmas presents under the tree?" Thus, to summarize, the combined problem-solving exchanges can be used to describe the *community-of-self* and cumulatively, to provide a personalized profile of the teacher candidate's situated engagement styles in the context of their self-defined views as an example of development.

REFERENCES

Bandura, A. (2006). Toward a psychology of human agency. *Perspectives on Psychological Science, 1*(2), 164–180.

Bronfenbrenner, U. (1986). Ecology of the family as a context for human development. *Research Perspectives, 22*(6), 723–742.

Guerra, N. S. (2001). *LIBRE Model.* Unpublished manuscript.

Guerra, N. S. (2006). The LIBRE problem-solving model: A practical approach to problem-solving and decision-making for teachers and teacher educators. *Texas Teacher Educator's Forum, 29*, 9–14.

Guerra, N. S. (2009). LIBRE stick figure tool: Graphic organizer. *Interventions in Schools and Clinics. 44*(4), 1–5.

Schunk, D. (1990). Goal setting and self-efficacy during self-regulated learning. *Educational Psychologist, 25*, 71–86.

Schunk, D. (2012). *Learning theories: An educational perspective.* Allyn & Bacon.

Stringer, E. T. (2007). *Action research* (3rd ed.). Sage Publications.

Vygotsky, L. (1978). *Mind in society: The development of higher psychological processes.* Harvard University Press.

Zimmerman, B. (2000). The development of scientific skills. *Development Review, 20*, 99–149.

CHAPTER 10

INITIAL AND SUSTAINED ATTENTION

Students enter the university with multiple identities, experiences, and assets that one day will be facets of their teaching (Jacobson et al., 2019). As educators, we can appreciate this complex view of learning and development. Thus, the foundation for this research which incorporated an examination of teacher preparation from the view of teacher candidates as "whole persons" juggling life with their aspirations, complex persons with the desire to become teachers. The goal is that once these students graduate, they will become the educational leaders who create change in classrooms, in schools, and in districts where they will be actively involved in developing policy. To close, it seems only fitting that we would review what we have discussed.

We began with teacher preparation to introduce a missing curriculum, that of social emotional learning moderated by strength-based problem-solving. We then introduced the LIBRE Model to explain the fluid role of attention, initial and sustained attention, to provide information about self-awareness, self-management, and responsible decision-making. We learned how engagement styles allowed for increased social awareness and motivational investment (Guerra, 2009) and the embracing of complexities that occur within and outside the educational experience (Jacobson et al., 2019). To address this ambitious goal, multiple method-

Teacher Candidate Problem-Solving Engagement Styles:
LIBRE Model Self-Management Analysis, pages 107–111.
Copyright © 2022 by Information Age Publishing
www.infoagepub.com
All rights of reproduction in any form reserved.

ological tools were implemented to capture the intricacies of the teacher candidate experiences found in the problem-solving. We examined the teacher candidates expressed insights into their career development and responsible decision making through their problem-solving. We acknowledged that neither curriculum nor students are one dimensional; demonstrated was the density of who they were and who they were becoming as they selected to embrace their learning opportunities with the intentional care to self through strength-based problem-solving; they incorporated their personal assets, resources, and skills and incorporated those strengths into their curricular experience-based problem-solving.

ENGAGEMENT MANAGEMENT

Social Emotional Learning in Problem-solving

Multiple researchers and the Collaborative for Academic, Social, and Emotional Learning (CASEL) organization contributed to over two decades of work for what is now described as social emotional learning skills; the five domains are self-awareness, self-management, social awareness, relational skills and intervening skill of responsible decision-making (1944). It is this decision-making domain, implemented in the problem-solving with the **LIBRE Model** and its scripted prompts that allow for the integrated contextualization. We opened with a discussion focused on attention to explain how problem-solving introduces a "pause" to move away from the automatic problem management tendencies, and to explore other self-management options. We examined the advantage of automaticity in allowing time efficiency and quick response, as well as its disadvantage when the process approach is not a match to the problem need. For instance, the teacher who always says "no," so he is distracted by requests. Unfortunately, there may also be a lost learning moment with the automatic response. We discussed self-awareness and self-monitoring as skills to facilitate goal management and minimize distractibility. We then explored the constructs of *initial* and *sustained attention*. **LIBRE Model** teacher candidate exchanges were presented to allow us to see the problem-solvers' pondering, the who, how and what they attended to as their problems were defined and managed (Guerra, 2015, 2016). We explored the multiple attention distractors that appeared within their daily life events and how they behaviorally carry-out their plans. To these points, we considered how the LIBRE Model was used to draw attention to the seesaw *features of attention;* that of attention and attention-withdraw exhibited as a continuous flow of individualized investment. We considered the value in processing challenge to introduce individual strengths. This observed as they embraced change and in response to challenge, new engagement style was practiced and emerged.

To provide a developmental context, we considered Erikson (1968) and Bronfenbrenner (1986), and reflected on the human experience. We addressed the importance of background information as assets to identity and to the discovery of possible conflicting identities. The examined intersectionality allowed us to see

Initial and Sustained Attention • **109**

the individual multiple "selves" that can then be combined in responding within multiple contexts. For instance, the student who is actively involved in learning and growing into new emerging identities; the self-awareness can be an additive benefit. Thus, the importance in self-investment.

The **LIBRE Model** provided problem-solving activity, facilitated and tracked *initial* and *sustained attention*. *Initial attention* is defined within the individual's social cognitive—environmental perception or worldviews, values, personal beliefs, and behaviors that are aligned with the self and how they interact with each of the other two factors. *Sustained attention* was defined in goal-oriented investment. Combined, the *initial* and *sustained attention*, provided the four distinct attention styles: ***potential engagement*** –not being engaged from beginning to end of the problem-solving; ***venting engagement*** –initial engagement that does not remain but rather drops off with not sustained investment in problem-solving; the ***goal-focused engagement*** –initial non-engagement that becomes engaged once a specific goal is identified within the problem-solving; and ***actual engagement***— initial and sustained engagement, remaining engaged throughout the entire problem-solving exchange (Guerra, 2009). We discussed how patterns of engagement and non-engagement associate with different contexts. All engagement styles have a purpose. Important to remember is that all engagement styles have a place in supporting and sustaining professional development; key is "how" and "when" to use specific engagement styles. At times, engagement styles operate as protective factors. The key is self-awareness in managing the *self* to create a matched engagement with the expectations of the context, setting, and culture.

The presented engagement theoretical framework allowed for the design of a personal psychosocial-cognitive learning system that includes the individual and their roles/identities, the consideration of context, and the multiple contexts that persons are moving in and out of over the course of a day. An example of these multiple roles and contexts is the individual who is a daughter at home, employee at work, and student at school.

We discussed the role of learning and how learning can be used to introduce and facilitate a proactive engagement (or not). And more importantly, we considered how teacher candidates must be given time and space to manage the multiple transitioning spaces. The time spent in considering, learning, and experiencing self-awareness impacted self-management for the teacher candidates involved in this problem-solving dialog. For those preparing teacher candidates for the profession, teachers must be taught the importance of including a holistic strategic design approach to learning that extends beyond the cognitive development of their students to include the whole person: social, cultural context, and psycho-emotional management (Guerra et al., 2009). The logical way of presenting this information is experientially; allowing them to learn first-hand about *self* as a person managing multiple identities and roles. This allows for ethical and professional development as each examines the facets and adaptations made.

110 • TEACHER CANDIDATE PROBLEM-SOLVING ENGAGEMENT STYLES

With the multiple approaches, we examined two teacher candidates as case studies and as illustrations of the APA multicultural ecological model in application with teachers. We then applied this identity/role intersectionality with the two teacher candidates with the examination of their multiple contexts and identities in the relational resilience. Each teacher candidate explored challenge as an individual-in-group, *community-of-self*, to better explore and understand their multiple views to self. The individual as a group parallel was made to encompass the intersectionality of a person; as the individual see's "self" holistically and with the multiple contexts and identity roles. In other words, there are distinctive voices, different beliefs or varied experiences that interact to comprise this examination of an individual-as-group. The complex exploration provides a much richer developmental detail. This presentation also gave an opportunity to examine individualized patterns of engagement-to-context-to-role identification. The purpose of this investigation to facilitate self-awareness toward more strategic self-regulation. The structure of action research provided an ideal approach for that exploration.

We revisited the importance of skill development. Attention and engagement styles are learned. As professional skills, they impact groomed development. The problem-solving participant data illustrated how problem-solving and understanding engagement styles can facilitate self-management. The goal was to suggest that attention can be strategically groomed, as with any skill, and implemented to match context to facilitate communication. To illustrate, imagine a person eating whatever and whenever the food is placed in front of him/her. The result is unmanaged eating. The same occurrence can be said of unmonitored attention; novelty draws the investment and there are no limits to distractibility. Namely, without the self-awareness or discipline, novelty will draw attention until the next novelty draws attention from the first. And of course, just as there are consequences to unregulated eating, there are consequences to unmanaged attention. Patterns of automaticity in eating and/or attention will likely produce similar random patterns in eating and/or attention. Conversely, attention that is self-managed will likely produce self-regulated change.

When we focus on different engagement style communications, this information is a resource and an additional asset to be acknowledged to better communicate and connect with each student. Each student is embraced as the complex individual of mind, body, and spirit. The holistically viewed self is valued; their engagement styles become patterns-in-development to which new context may be introduced to teach new engagement styles. All students are viewed as "haves" rather than "have-nots" and what each has is a "strength."

Strength-based strategies are limitless. Examining the engagement style preferences in relation to context provides yet an additional strength-based tactic for introducing the intersectionality to the view of individual-as-group. The development of individuals is complex. Thus, when the complexity of development is considered, and studied, it can be found to inform and provide opportunity for individuals to manage and monitor their own strategic design engagement. Self-awareness is attention that can then be used to teach teachers skills that not only facilitate their teaching, but also teach them how to better connect and value their students' engagement and various backgrounds and contextual experiences.

REFERENCES

Bronfenbrenner, U. (1986). Ecology of the family as a context for human development: *Research perspectives. Developmental psychology, 22*(6), 723–742.

Collaborative for Academic, Social, and Emotional Learning (CASEL). (1994). https://casel.org/what-is-sel/

Erikson, E. (1968). *Identity: Youth and crisis*. Norton.

Guerra, N. S. (2009). Illustrations of engagement styles: Four teacher candidates. *Teacher Education & Practice, 22*(1), 95–117.

Guerra, N. S. (2015). *Clinical problem-solving case management.* Rowan & Littlefield and Lexington Books.

Guerra, N. S. (2016). *Addressing challenges Latinos/as encounter with the LIBRE Model: Listen-identify-brainstorm-reality-test-encourage.* Peter Lang Publishing.

Guerra, N. S., Flores, B. B., & Claeys, L. (2009). A case study of an induction year teacher's problem-solving using the LIBRE Model. *New Horizons in Education, Journal of Education, 57*(1), 43–57.

Jacobson, M. J., Levin, J. A., & Kapur, M. (2019). Education as a complex system: Conceptual and methodological implications. *Educational Researcher, 48*(2), 112–119.

GLOSSARY

Actual engagement—problem-solver is detailed and specific in exploration of options and resolutions to the LIBRE Model; individual is observed as reflective and attentive

Affordance—an experience between the person and their environments that provides advantage to developmental agility

Attention—multifaceted function of intentional and/or responsive thought

Attention-distraction seesaw—heightened thought demands-on-time with increased consequence and impact; the combined increase in distractibility and attention demand

Automatic attention (automaticity)—the unthinking attention allocated to experienced stimuli

Client development—life span self-awareness and LIBRE Model feedback to facilitate intervention management

Community-of-Self—multiple roles, identities, and context; and how the reciprocal interactions impact one-to-the-other to produce different engagement investments

Ecosystem—factors that compliment social and personal development

Engagement—an observable and behavioral manifestation

Teacher Candidate Problem-Solving Engagement Styles:
LIBRE Model Self-Management Analysis, pages 113–114.
Copyright © 2022 by Information Age Publishing
www.infoagepub.com
All rights of reproduction in any form reserved.

114 • TEACHER CANDIDATE PROBLEM-SOLVING ENGAGEMENT STYLES

Engagement styles—combination of Initial and Sustained attention problem-solver response patterns; four combinations emerge as different levels of attention

Engagement profile (EP)—multiple roles, identities(culture, values), context, in reciprocal interaction one-with-the-other to produce a defined personalized EP

Goal-focused engagement—problem-solver is solution-oriented; not interested in exploring the context of the problem rather the investment is to the resolution

Identity—presented as context for personal and professional development

Initial Attention—language-investment in problem-oriented social context, brainstorming resolution options, and the reality testing of the generated options

LIBRE Model—problem solving activity; the acronym for L-listen, I-identify a problem, B-brainstorm resolution options, R-reality test, E-encourage, is used to identify problem-solvers responses

Managed engagement—the adaptability required to move from one social setting to another

Potential engagement—individual has selected not to engage in problem solving; filtering self

Professional development—self-investment and ongoing practicing of learned and refined specialized skills

Self-actualization—Maslow's (1943) hierarchical needs presentation, in which he asserts that all individuals are motivated to become self-actualized. A condition in which one is self-aware and allocates attention to altruism and selfishness

Self-efficacy—how one sees and assesses self in relation to the identified task which functions as the goal

Self-reflection—willingness to self-examine personal and/or professional thoughts, plans, and/or actions

Self-regulation—self-management of cognitive and behavioral actions/inactions

Social cognitive theory—Bandura's reciprocal relation between the individual, behavior, and environment involving interaction of being a product and process of systems

Soft skills—relational communication skills, responsibility, motivation, teamwork, leadership, problem-solving

Sustained Attention—problem-solvers' continued investment to focus on an identified challenge up to the development of a resolution

Venting engagement—problem-solver exhibits a shorter attentive investment, reflected in the explanation and context of the problem however with no interest in exploring a resolution

Printed in the United States
by Baker & Taylor Publisher Services